Daily Journals

CAROL SIMPSON

ILLUSTRATED BY YOSHI MIYAKE

Dedication

I wish to dedicate this book to my family for their patience during my long hours of ignoring them while I wrote this book!

GoodYearBooks

are available for most basic curriculum subjects plus many enrichment areas. For more GoodYearBooks, contact your local bookseller or educational dealer. For a complete catalog with information about other GoodYearBooks, please write:

GoodYearBooks
ScottForesman
1900 East Lake Avenue
Glenview, IL 60025

Design by Karen Kohn & Associates.
Copyright © 1993 Carol Simpson.
All Rights Reserved.
Printed in the United States of America

3 4 5 6 7 8 9 - ER - 01 00 99 98 97 96 95 94 93

ISBN 0-673-36062-8

PREFACE

My experience with children and writing began during my second or third teaching year. I told the children that I wanted them to write something for me. Before that, they had never been asked to write anything more than their names, spelling words, fill-in-the-blank worksheets, and similar materials. Choosing their own words in their minds and putting those words on paper was a new idea for these children. I am afraid that I was skeptical about the results of the task. My skepticism was based on the assumptions that six-year-olds don't know how to spell many words and don't really have anything to say anyway. Was I wrong!

That first writing assignment came the morning after a big snowfall. The students had been listening to poetry about winter for several days. I was pleased that they could understand the poets' sometimes vague messages. I decided that my students would each write a poem about snow.

I wish that I had saved the results. They were really wonderful! The children wrote anywhere from two to six lines, most with rhyme. Some wrote very nice descriptive phrases. Everyone tried to write something. I was so pleased that I put the children's poems together in a "big book" that they could read in their free time. And read it they did. That big book of poems quickly became one of their favorites.

Since that first experience with creative writing, I have had my students put pencil to paper often. I have tried giving specific assignments, but I have also allowed my students to come up with their own ideas for writing. Both methods accomplish the objective: expecting the children to write about something.

The idea of writing "daily journals" was addressed by several presenters at a reading conference I attended several years

MEGAN

ago. All of the people who had tried this form of writing seemed pleased with it. I made up my mind that I would squeeze the time into my schedule and include it daily. Surely it would be better than the occasional writing my students would do when time and subject presented itself easily. The decision to change to daily journals was one of the best I've made.

In this book, you will find ideas from kindergarten, first-, second-, and third-grade classrooms where daily journals have already proven to be successful. These teachers use some form of daily writing in their classes, and they have shared some of their best ideas and practices with me so that I might present them to you. You will find suggestions for using journals as a way of teaching proper written language usage. The term "journals" will be used to refer to written materials produced by the students, whether the subject is one of their own choosing or one assigned by the teacher.

At the end of the book, you will find an appendix that contains examples of students' writing. These writing samples play an important part in showing how much progress can be made in a year (in some cases, in just a matter of weeks or months) when children are allowed time to write every day. The examples also show some of the creative ability that surfaces when students are challenged to create stories on their own.

It is exciting to see how daily writing is catching on; teachers who have tried it and have seen successful results are urging their colleagues to include it, too. I hope that you will try it, and that you will experience your own successes.

ACKNOWLEDGEMENTS

Thank you to Linda Cope, Susan Bailey, Elise Sgro, and many other whole-language teachers for sharing ideas. Their input helped make this book possible.

I also would like to thank the following young authors, whose work appears throughout the book. Without their efforts, I could not show what can be accomplished with persistence in journal writing. And a special thanks to their parents, who gave permission for such usage.

Brandon Bowman	Ryan Glasnovich	Reid Peachey
Alex Boyden	Stuart Jeckel	Mike Peterson
Lindsey Dechert	Megan Johnson	Melinda Stickle
Erin Glasnovich	Kelly McGunnigal	Brian Tucker
	Mary Park	

ERIN

CONTENTS

BRIAN

BRANDON

From *Daily Journals*, published by GoodYearBooks. Copyright © 1993 Carol Simpson.

ALEX

ALEX

From *Daily Journals*, published by GoodYearBooks. Copyright © 1993 Carol Simpson.

INTRODUCTION

No one will argue against the idea that everyone needs to have learned certain basic skills, such as reading and writing, by the time he or she finishes his or her formal education. Every teacher, regardless of the subject or grade level, should strive to improve his or her students' ability to read and comprehend the subject being taught. Writing, on the other hand, is often put aside for other more important curricular responsibilities. By not expecting our students to show their ability to write correct sentences, are we not reducing the importance of this basic life skill?

Writing, as a subject, needs to be taught in kindergarten and then proceed year after year throughout a child's formal education. The best way to teach this skill is to begin early and then expect to see gradual improvement throughout the school experience. No teacher should feel that writing is not part of his or her curriculum, just as reading and comprehending should be included in all areas. Every teacher can and should expect students to write paragraphs or stories that explain what they are learning in class!

ERIN

HOW TO BEGIN

First, it is important to determine which students have written journals before coming to your classroom. Although the idea of journal writing is catching on and spreading rapidly, it is not safe to assume that every child has had the experience.

Kindergarten teachers whose students have gone to preschool might be surprised to discover that many children come to school having already drawn pictures and dictated (or even tried to "write") stories to accompany their pictures. This activity

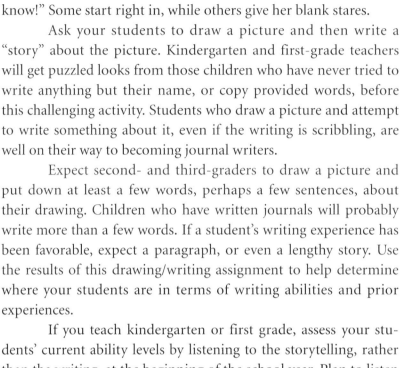

is a good starting point for getting students to write what will be called "journals."

Begin by asking, "Who has ever written a story?" The responses will help you determine how much students already know and how much will be new to them. One wise elementary teacher who wants to get her young students writing from the first day says she tells her first-graders to "write down everything you know!" Some start right in, while others give her blank stares.

Ask your students to draw a picture and then write a "story" about the picture. Kindergarten and first-grade teachers will get puzzled looks from those children who have never tried to write anything but their name, or copy provided words, before this challenging activity. Students who draw a picture and attempt to write something about it, even if the writing is scribbling, are well on their way to becoming journal writers.

Expect second- and third-graders to draw a picture and put down at least a few words, perhaps a few sentences, about their drawing. Children who have written journals will probably write more than a few words. If a student's writing experience has been favorable, expect a paragraph, or even a lengthy story. Use the results of this drawing/writing assignment to help determine where your students are in terms of writing abilities and prior experiences.

If you teach kindergarten or first grade, assess your students' current ability levels by listening to the storytelling, rather than the writing, at the beginning of the school year. Plan to listen for the use of complete sentences and correct sequencing when your students tell their stories. Do they use correct verb tenses when speaking? You will look much more closely at their written language by the time the children have completed a year of journal writing in your classroom.

If you teach second or third grade, when determining the current levels of your students, check those skills that previous teachers also assessed, namely use of complete sentences, correct sequencing of events, and use of proper verb tense. Add to these the use of proper capitalization and punctuation as well as the ability to write more complex sentences.

Introduce your students to the term "journal" by explaining that they are going to be writing words and sentences every day in a special file or notebook. Kindergarten teachers need to

From *Daily Journals*, published by GoodYearBooks. Copyright © 1993 Carol Simpson.

explain that the children will draw a picture every day and then try to put down words that tell what they draw. Students will soon get use to the idea of daily journal writing. Those who have had the experience before will have little trouble in continuing the activity; those who have not done it before will soon follow the routine and just might find it to be an enjoyable part of their day!

CLASSROOM ATMOSPHERE

Atmosphere in the journal writing classroom needs to be relaxed. While children write, they need to feel free to share what they are doing with those people who sit near them. If a child is writing a story about something that happened on the playground at recess, he or she will want the people whose names appear in the story to know that they are included. Obviously, loud talking is disturbing to others. Whispering should be encouraged during those times when children need to speak to others.

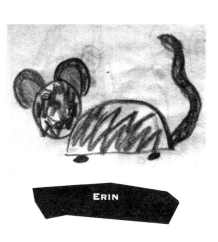

ERIN

Play classical or easy listening music while the children are writing in their journals. You will find children who enjoy (and find inspiration in) the music. Others never really hear it as they work. When the music stops, everyone should put away their work quietly and go on to something else. This can result in a very smooth transition from one subject to another. If you have the children share their journals immediately after writing, the end of the music can signal time to put away work (unless a child is sharing today) and meet on the rug or whatever location has been designated for sharing, to hear what fellow students are writing.

Remember that the important part of journal writing is the act of putting down one's thoughts in proper sentence form, in an order that makes sense. Part of the relaxed atmosphere must also include relaxed expectations with regard to spelling and handwriting. Children will not feel free to produce good stories if they are reprimanded for incorrect spelling or poor penmanship. The words "sloppy copy" are quite appropriate for what appears in a daily journal. Besides, if a child is going to share a story with others by putting it in a book, he or she will correct the spelling and messy penmanship.

You may find that you have to re-educate your parents. They may be more apt to reprimand for spelling errors and sloppy penmanship than you might expect. Perhaps a note at the beginning of the year that explains what you are going to be doing (and expecting from students) will help alleviate possible future difficulties.

Overall, remember that all students, regardless of age, need to be expected to put pencil and crayons to paper during journal writing time. Everyone needs to understand that this is not the time to horse around with friends. Journal writing is serious business, just as math or science.

TEACHERS AS ROLE MODELS

The atmosphere established during writing time helps the development of positive attitudes toward these language experiences. Demonstrate writing as a fun thing to do. Teachers need to be involved in the writing process as well. During journal time it is important that you try to spend some time writing in your own file or notebook. Students in kindergarten through third grade are still young enough to want to please the teacher. They still think that if you find pleasure in an activity, they will like to do it also! It's too bad that this attitude fades somewhere down the line. By writing and sharing what is written, teachers can be a powerful motivator for the children. What you share (it might be a story, a poem, even a grocery list) is not as important as the example you set for the students in the classroom.

HOW MUCH TIME SHOULD I ALLOW?

The amount of time you assign to journal writing will depend upon several factors. First, you need to examine your daily schedule to find those blocks of time that are flexible. Obviously, you must consider variables such as how much time is spent in other classrooms. Are there places you must be at specific times of the day? Once you have determined a usable block of time, consider this: Will you be allowing your students time to share immediately after writing? Sharing, as you will see, is an important function of writing, especially in the earlier grades.

Yet another factor to consider is whether or not it is going to be necessary to introduce a lesson before the writing takes place. If an introduction is needed, allow time for that as well as for the actual writing. The amount of time spent on the actual

ALEX

writing will depend upon the grade level you teach. Consider these suggestions:

K—1: Allow 15 minutes for writing and 15 minutes for sharing

Gr. 2: Allow 20-25 minutes for writing, 10 minutes for sharing

Gr. 3: Allow 25-30 minutes for writing, sharing is optional

The "optional" sharing mentioned for third-graders, although an important part of writing, will depend upon time constraints that seem to increase with each grade level. (See page 13 for some suggestions on how to include sharing even in the busiest schedule.)

Once the routine of pleasurable writing has found a place in your classroom, you will be surprised how many of your children will opt to write in their journals during "free choice" times. You may find that your children actually choose to write for more than the suggested time allotments because they want to work in their journals whenever they can.

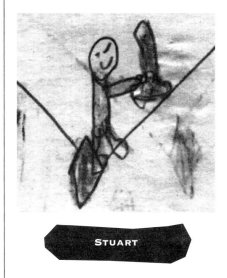

STUART

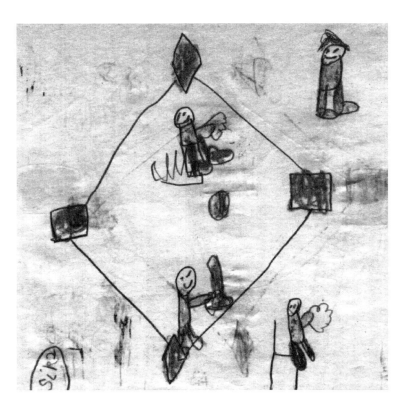

ABOUT JOURNALS

TYPES OF JOURNALS

A brief discussion of some of the many types of journals may help you decide which would be appropriate for your students.

PERSONAL JOURNALS

A child's personal journal is just that, personal. The child makes a choice about what to write in this journal. He or she may write about what happened during gym class; the topic might be a make-believe monster that resembles something the child saw on television; or, if a new baby is on the way, the child may write a story on that subject. There are no limitations, other than using good taste.

SMALL-GROUP OR WHOLE-CLASS JOURNALS

There may be occasions when you will want to allow either a small group of students or the entire class to write about a specific subject. Each student has his or her own page to write/draw a response to a story, event, or thematic unit. Either have everyone write at the same time and then combine the results, or give an entire blank journal to those who need to contribute a page, each one being able to see what has been done before his or her turn.

REACTION JOURNALS

Reaction journals are journals that children write as a reaction to literature that they either hear you read or read themselves. A reaction journal is more than a book report, although there will

MEGAN

be some similarities. Instead of writing just a synopsis of a book, the child must react, either favorably or not, to what is happening in the story. It can also relate to personal experiences.

MATH JOURNALS

Like the reaction journal, this journal is a response, but to a math lesson. You can get a good idea of who does or does not understand a given concept by asking the students to write their own descriptions of how to do a specific problem. Ask the children to write down, in their own words, how they arrived at their answer or ask the children to write down how to play a certain math game that the class has learned. Not only does this type of journal require that the student show his or her knowledge of written language, it also examines the understanding of mathematical concepts.

GRADE-APPROPRIATENESS OF JOURNAL TYPES

Kindergarten: Personal journals are the most appropriate for this age group; however, there may be times when whole-class journals are useful, such as upon completion of a thematic unit of study or a shared reading experience.

1st grade: Use personal journals on a daily basis throughout the entire school year. Whole-class and small-group journals may be useful on occasion and will not necessarily be written during journal writing time; instead, they may be assigned during reading class time. Introduce literature reaction journals later on in the school year. If you read chapter books to your students, ask the children to respond on paper after completion of a particularly interesting story. Or, if you are reading a good mystery, ask for predictions of what might happen next. Also, students can write reactions after the class finishes a basal. Ask them to compare/contrast two favorite or similar stories they have read.

2nd/3rd grade: These students can write a combination of all types of journals—whatever is appropriate for the situation. Personal journals are still important enough to consider using on a regular basis.

MARY

MAKING PERSONAL JOURNALS

There are many ways to put journals together. Often, the only materials needed are those that you already have at your disposal. To put journals together in the simplest form, staple together several sheets of paper to make a booklet. The type of paper you use will vary depending upon grade level.

PLAIN-PAPER STAPLED JOURNALS

Use this type to introduce journals. Kindergarten and beginning first-graders do well when you give them about five sheets of plain newsprint, stapled along the left side, to make a booklet. Distribute these on a Monday morning and let the children keep them in desks or storage places for use each day for one week. At the end of the week, collect these plain-paper journals. It is a good idea to try to save a selection of student journals from various times in the year for comparison at parent/teacher conferences. Have students put the date on each journal, either on Monday mornings or on Fridays when they are finished and collected. Even kindergartners can be taught to date their journals each time.

Five- and six-year-olds need plain paper because, in most cases, the pictures they draw are a very important part of the journal. Many cannot write words as yet; their pictures are the basis for stories that they tell during sharing. Writing stories to read comes later.

Five-page plain-paper journals work well throughout the kindergarten year. They work well during the first couple of months in first grade also. The time for a change is when you notice that the children are trying to write more words and sentences about the pictures they draw in their personal journals each day.

PICTURE STORY® PAPER JOURNALS

Picture Story® paper, which is available at most teacher supply stores, has drawing space as well as writing lines. A "cover" of construction paper and two to three sheets of 9" x 12" Picture Story® paper, side stapled, provides an adequate supply of writing space for one week in a first-grade classroom. Once again the pictures play a very important part of the journal writing. Continue Monday distribution and Friday collection (and dating) until the children begin telling you that they are not finished with their

MARY

"story" by Friday, or when they say they need more paper in their journal to finish a story. Then it is time to add more paper.

First-grade teachers may find that Picture Story® paper journals perform an important function. By mid-October, you should expect those children who have been drawing pictures and not trying to write words in their personal journals to begin making sentences, or at least words and phrases, about their illustrations. By giving them paper with writing lines, you will give most a hint to put down words. Even reluctant writers will try to write because of the negative reaction of their peers when they share a journal with empty lines. Peer pressure will force them to try and write a story.

LONGER JOURNALS

It is time to put more sheets of Picture Story® paper in children's journals when they indicate either that they don't have enough room to finish their story or that they have not finished writing their story by the Friday collection time. When this happens, you'll know that they are attempting to write more words. Their stories will become more detailed and have more interesting plots that require more time to write. When this change takes place, put more sheets of Picture Story® paper in the journal and change the distribution/collection routine. Instead of a Monday to Friday schedule, children will help themselves to a new journal when they need one. They will date their completed journals and turn them in when finished. This means that you need to keep a supply of new journals on hand at all times. This type of journal works well for the remainder of the first-grade year.

WRITING FOLDERS

If you teach second grade, you might choose to start the year with six or seven pages of Picture Story® paper in a "cover" for personal journals. After the first few weeks, students get accustomed to writing journals. Then you can give them file folders in which to store their writing.

Because many second-graders begin reading chapter books, with fewer illustrations, they do not take as great an interest in drawing pictures for their own stories. They may prefer to write their stories on the regular classroom writing paper. Rather than staple several pages together to make a booklet, wait for the

ERIN

From *Daily Journals*, published by GoodYearBooks. Copyright © 1993 Carol Simpson.

student to report that he or she has finished a story. Then staple the pages together in correct sequence. Remind the child to write down the date for later reference.

Many second-grade teachers often want to assign special writing topics on story-starter papers. These can easily be stored in a student's file folder with his or her personal journal writing. Second-graders are, hopefully, organized enough that they do not lose the pages they write, but can keep them together in their folder. Once a week, or when necessary, collect the folders and read through the journal work, as well as the assigned stories, pulling out what is needed for a random evaluation of a student's writing progress.

An important feature of the single sheets of paper used in this type of writing folder is that the children can select the kind of paper they wish to use. Keep a ready supply of classroom handwriting paper as well as some 9" x 12" Picture Story® paper so that those children who want to make a drawing will have appropriate paper for their needs. Remember, the relaxed unpressured atmosphere during writing time is enhanced when children feel comfortable—even down to the kind of paper they like to use.

ALEX

SPIRAL NOTEBOOKS

Third-grade teachers need to request that students bring a spiral notebook to school along with their usual school supplies. Using spiral notebooks as personal journals has several advantages. First, there is less need to provide several kinds of paper because third-graders, as a rule, are less interested in illustrating their stories first. They take more time in writing the words. They need less drawing room. If they wish to draw, they will do it on the lined paper with no problem. Second, spiral notebooks provide plenty of paper. Stories can be kept in the notebook for the entire school year. Last, the paper is attached to the book, so it is harder to lose papers. This makes it easier for you to collect, read, and respond to what the students are writing on a routine schedule. Spiral notebooks are also useful for math journals.

Responding is a very important part of writing these journals, so be sure to collect and respond at least once a week. Read the child's work and then respond to it by writing a note to the student. By keeping all stories in the spiral notebook, you can review the child's work, and your own comments about it, at any time.

When you use story starters, ask the students to write their stories, cut them to size, and paste them inside the pages of the spiral notebook. This way, all writing assignments will be within easy grasp when needed. Give parents the notebook at conference time so they can read the stories and your comments.

STORY COLLECTIONS

Small-group or whole-class stories can often be made on paper that has been cut to a specific shape, depending on the subject (such as a pumpkin shape for a Halloween story collection or an egg shape for a collection of Easter stories). These are called "story starters." You can combine story-starter papers in a class collection and staple them together with a cover of construction paper, provided that all students have used a consistent size or shape of writing paper.

There may be times when you want to display the children's stories in the classroom. To do so, staple the stories to a large, appropriate shape made of tagboard or colored poster paper. For example, if you give the children a circular shape of paper for writing stories, you could staple all of these circles in the center of a large bear shape. The circles could represent the bear's tummy.

Using the bear shape idea, students write their stories on standard-sized paper. Give the children another piece of paper with a bear shape on it. Ask the children to decorate the paper with colorful clothes that the bear might wear. Attach the story-starter paper behind the bear's clothes. Open the bear's shirt, and read the story.

Last, you can make accordion books with pages folded like a paper fan cut in circle shapes. Fasten the shapes together to make a bookworm.

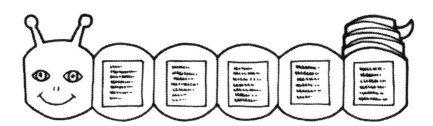

From *Daily Journals*, published by GoodYearBooks. Copyright © 1993 Carol Simpson.

Reaction journals also make nice class or small-group collections. To facilitate making the class collection later, be sure that all students use a standard paper or form for the writing assignment.

Taking Time to Share

For kindergartners and first-graders, it is especially important to share what is being written in personal journals. Students at this age are anxious to show what they can do. They have no inhibitions, yet, about getting up in front of a group of their peers and showing off. For them, the idea of sharing what they write is a natural part of journal writing. And it is best done immediately after the writing has taken place, while stories are fresh in their minds.

The experience of sharing journals aloud needs to be continued in second grade, but this might be done less frequently—perhaps once a week. At that time, those students who have completed a story or those who desire peer feedback might volunteer to share aloud. Be sure that everyone is included at least once a month. Try buddy sharing (reading a journal to a friend) as well.

By third grade, students are becoming more self-conscious about sharing their writing in front of their peers. For some children, sharing is more embarrassing than it is fun. If you choose to omit the sharing time from the daily schedule, do so with confidence if you are writing in your students' spiral notebooks on a regular basis. Each child will get the feedback that is given during sharing; it will be teacher feedback, not peer feedback.

Scheduling

At the beginning of the year teachers of kindergarten and first grade may want to take the time to allow everyone who wants to to share their journal every day. A simple "Who would like to show us what they are writing in their journal?" will result in a flurry of waving hands. "I do! I do!" will be the response. The five- and six-year-olds are anxious to show and tell what they can do.

There is not enough time in the school year to allow everyone to share every day. It will become necessary to streamline the sharing process after a week or two. To solve the problem of everyone wanting to share, you might organize the number of students in your class into four or five small groups. Each day one

MARY

of these small groups will share their journals. Write names of the students in each group on cards for all to see. Rotate the cards each day so that everyone in class shares at least once a week.

BUDDY SHARING

For second- and third-grade teachers who can't take the time from busy schedules to allow sharing every day, an easy alternative is to try buddy sharing. Have the children share in pairs or groups of three. Each child must read his or her journal to a buddy; the buddy must listen and ask questions about the story. If everyone shares with a buddy at the same time, it only requires 5 to 10 minutes. It does tend to get a little noisy, however, when all buddy groups are reading at the same time, but the amount of noisy time is minimal. Buddy sharing is not required every day—it can be scheduled once a week.

Get input from the buddy sharing by asking questions at the end of the session: Who heard a funny story? Who heard a true story? Did anyone hear their own name in a story being shared by a buddy? Has anyone written a story about a turkey or leprechaun, or whatever topic might have been suggested for the season or holiday? You encourage good listening on the part of the buddies when you ask such questions immediately after the sharing takes place.

THE BENEFITS OF SHARING

Taking the time to allow the students to share has its benefits. Sharing is a good way to practice the language arts skills of listening and speaking. The benefits of sharing journal writing orally are worthy of the time it takes to do the task.

STUDENTS SHARE FEELINGS Even very shy students should be expected to share on a regular schedule. Shy students will often express feelings that they hold inside themselves when they write stories. By using story characters, they can say what they would not usually say directly to their classmates. A child who is shy and lonely can tell through a story character how it feels to have few friends. The child who lacks friends because of inappropriate behavior can write a story about how he or she feels inside. It is then easier for his or her peers to comment on the story character's behavior and suggest ways to be a better friend. One child who wrote about how it felt to never get asked to help

MEGAN

From *Daily Journals*, published by GoodYearBooks. Copyright © 1993 Carol Simpson.

distribute birthday treats got a positive response from her journal story. She was asked to help with treats on the very next birthday.

STUDENTS SHARE THEIR WRITING IDEAS When students share their journals, they get to hear what others are writing. They get ideas for their own journals. Some children need to hear from others' stories to gain confidence that what they themselves are writing is acceptable. Also, students need to hear peer reactions to what they are writing. They need to hear their audience's laughter when something is funny. They need to see the surprised look in the audience's eyes when something unexpected happens in the story.

PEER PRESSURE TO PERFORM Every classroom contains a handful of students who do not perform up to expectations. This is often the case with journal writing. There are those children who you know could do more if they would just put their minds to it. No matter how many suggestions you make, they just don't seem to want to *do* more.

The best pressure to perform comes from the students' peers. When students share their journals on a regular basis, the young audience is aware of what was heard the last time, and it has certain expectations about what should be heard now.

The child who has not been writing many (or any) words on his or her journal page and who has been telling rather than reading the story during sharing time will be pressured to write something. The audience, they will soon discover, wants to hear the words on their page. There are children who can tell a great story about their illustrations. But because the other children are trying to write a good story, they expect everyone else to do the same. In order to get a positive peer response the child must read, not tell, stories.

LEARNING TO LISTEN AND QUESTION You as the teacher need to model the job of listener and critic. As a child is sharing a journal entry, you need to demonstrate being a good listener by giving full attention to the reader. Then demonstrate the technique of questioning: "What will happen next?" or "Does this sentence go with the rest of the story?" At the end of the reading, ask the audience what the author's main idea is in the story. Ask for the audience's favorite page or illustration.

You must also model the technique of making suggestions. If a child has written sentences that represent a good begin-

KELLY

ning, show the students how to make suggestions to complete a story: "Why don't you write about what happens when . . . ." If the author has sentences with a repetitious pattern ("I like . . .) suggest that they continue with it and create an "I Like . . ." book. Students who are learning to be good listeners will soon catch on to the questioning techniques and will begin asking their own. They will also want to start making suggestions to the author. You may be surprised at some of the good suggestions they can make! Teacher guides to basal readers always include questions and predictions about stories in the reader. Use some of the same techniques when reading journal stories and you will show your students that there is a practical application of the listening/questioning skills in a real-life situation.

STORING JOURNALS

Don't expect kindergartners to keep their journals for longer than a week at a time. At the end of the week, collect the journals. Send old journals home regularly, or save a selection of them from various times during the year.

First-graders keep their journals in their desks until they have finished writing their stories. At that time, collect the journals. Often the children will want to refer to what they have written in an older journal. For this reason, journals need to be kept in the classroom in a place where the children can find them. Plastic crates that can accommodate box-bottom hanging files are good. Each child has his or her name on the tab of a box-bottom file. All work is kept in that file so that the child can gain access to it.

Expect second-graders who keep a file folder in their desks for their writing papers to keep all work together for at least a month at a time. Once a month children can clean their files and give you everything but the stories they are currently writing. Save the writing or send it home after examination and evaluation.

There should be no storage problem for third-grade teachers whose students are using spiral notebooks to write their personal journals. The students keep their journals in their desks for the entire year. Story-starter papers that are not pasted into spiral notebooks can be stored in manilla folders or hanging files in crates.

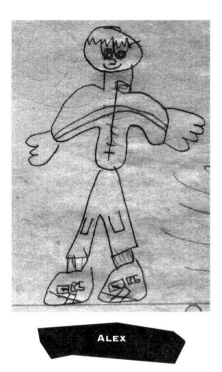

ALEX

From *Daily Journals,* published by GoodYearBooks. Copyright © 1993 Carol Simpson.

SUBJECT MATTER: WHAT DO WE WRITE?

You might be surprised to find that children usually know what they want to write. If you give them the paper they usually don't sit for very long before they begin writing, or at least drawing the picture that they will then write sentences to describe. Once in a while you need to channel their writing activity into a certain mold or genre.

One kindergarten teacher reads *Harold and the Purple Crayon* by Crockett Johnson before her children begin journal writing. The idea of the story is that Harold can draw anything—there are no limitations. Students will understand this idea about their journal entries if they hear about Harold before the writing experience begins. (You need not be a kindergarten teacher to get this idea across to your children!)

SUGGESTIONS FOR RELUCTANT WRITERS

Those students who might be called "reluctant writers" are the least motivated to begin on their own. They lack confidence in their ability to write a story until they meet with success a time or two. There are some easy topics that reluctant writers might use to help them get started. Finding success in writing a story is difficult for those students who lack confidence. The following suggestions are designed to help build confidence because they can result in a "book" such as the children might find in their school library.

MARY

GROUP BOOKS

Reluctant writers can usually feel successful by participating in a group book. It is helpful to write a story that is based on a book

MARY

the group has just read together. Books with a simple story line and repetitive phrases are easy to duplicate with some minor changes. Each group member writes a page in the book. You can put it together and duplicate it, and each group member can have a copy to read and take home.

There are many stories that have repetitive patterns which work well for this kind of project. Bill Martin, Jr.'s *Brown Bear, Brown Bear, What Do You See?* is a good example of a book with a repetitive pattern that works well here. Kindergarten and first-grade teachers will find it very useful; second-grade teachers with students who have had very little prior experience in writing may find it useful early in the school year. Because of the pattern that repeats itself page after page, this type of writing assignment may not be appropriate for third-graders.

A simple variation on the group book is the class book. In this project, everyone in class creates one page. Projects of this type just beg to be put together in a "big book" format, perhaps in a simple shape that deals with the story's theme. If you are writing "Pumpkin, Pumpkin, What Do You See?", you might give everyone a page in the shape of a large pumpkin. If the students are writing ghost stories, you might make big ghost-shaped pages. If everyone is completing the sentence "Happiness is . . . ," the shape of a teddy bear might be appropriate.

To put these big books together, you need only punch holes along the left side and put the pages together with binding rings. Each child should be allowed to take the class book home for an overnight visit so that it might be read to family members. The children can point to their own pages with pride.

ALPHABET BOOKS

Depending upon the requirements you make for the detail of the sentences, an alphabet book would be applicable to all grade levels, K-3. Kindergarten teachers can suggest that their students write only the letters and try to match pictures with the appropriate beginning sound. First-grade teachers can ask students to write simple sentences, such as "A is for apple. B is for bear." Second-grade teachers can require an action in the sentence: "Apples are to eat. Bears like to sleep all winter." By adding the requirement of adjectives, the third-grade teacher can make the assignment more appropriate for that level: "A is for apple. Apples are to eat. Apples are juicy."

The alphabet book is no longer a book for beginning readers—or writers. *Animalia* by Graeme Base is an example of just how complex an alphabet book can become. Jerry Pallotta's alphabet books are good for specific topics in an a-b-c format, a tough one to write. *Q Is for Duck* by Mary Elting and Michael Folsom offers a different kind of alphabet book, one of predicting what is on the next page.

NUMBER BOOKS

Just as with the alphabet books, teachers can change the requirements of a number book to match the grade level. Beginning writers simply write a numeral or number word and draw a corresponding picture. Expect older students to write sentences with nouns, then verbs, and then adverbs or adjectives, or both. Tailor your suggestions to the writer. *Fish Eyes: A Book You Can Count On* by Lois Ehlert or *The Doorbell Rang* by Pat Hutchins are good examples of easy to difficult number-book styles.

COLOR WORD BOOKS

Another suggestion that could be applied to K-3 grade levels is a color word book. Kindergarten teachers should require that a color word match the color used in the picture on the page. Extend that to writing a complete sentence in first grade, add a complex sentence in second grade, and an even more complex sentence in third grade. Even reluctant writers will find success in trying to write color word stories.

BOOKS ABOUT TIME

The Very Hungry Caterpillar by Eric Carle is an example of a days-of-the-week story. *Chicken Soup with Rice* by Maurice Sendak, although difficult, is a good example of a story based on the months of the year. *A House for Hermit Crab* by Eric Carle is much simpler. Time (hour by hour) is the progressive theme in *The Grouchy Ladybug* by Eric Carle. Each of these predictable themes is a good beginning for first-, second-, or third-graders who want to write but cannot think up a good plot.

WORDLESS PICTURE BOOKS

Just as the name implies, there are no words in this type of story, just illustrations. Because the child does not have to use written

MEGAN

language, this may be applicable to only kindergarten or first-graders. Wordless picture books require good sequencing skills. They allow the student to practice storytelling skills.

WRITING A STORY TO MATCH ILLUSTRATIONS

A variation on the wordless picture book is a story written to match given illustrations. Reluctant writers might be given several pictures that show specific events in a familiar story. Cutting old workbooks will provide illustrations from basal stories that the student has read. Ask the child to sequence several pictures and then write a story that matches them. Depending upon the detail in the illustrations, this activity could be appropriate for first through third grades. Once again, the reluctant writer does not have to think of a plot or sequence of events on his own.

SUGGESTIONS FOR SIMPLE WRITING TOPICS

Those students who do not want to rely on specific ideas (alphabet, color word, number word books, and others mentioned above), but want to create their own stories, can try writing stories about things they know best.

"I CAN . . ." STORIES

This simple idea results in any number of pages of sentences that begin with "I can . . . ." First-graders might be satisfied with simple sentences such as "I can run fast." By second and third grade, expect that sentence to be more complex; perhaps contain the word "because" as well as adjectives and adverbs: "I can run very fast because I exercise my body every day."

FRIENDS AND FAMILY

Students can write stories about their friends and what they do together to have fun. Family becomes a good topic because the children can write about their moms and dads, brothers and sisters, pets, homes, and what families do together to have a good time. The list goes on and on. Friends and families are excellent topics for those students who have difficulty creating a plot and sequence of events.

MARY

From *Daily Journals*, published by GoodYearBooks. Copyright © 1993 Carol Simpson.

TRUE-LIFE STORIES

These stories are not necessarily descriptions of events that reflect friends and/or family. They can be about feelings such as fear when having to visit the doctor's office; jealousy about a new baby in the house; excitement about a birthday present; or anger at siblings. True-life stories are appropriate at any grade level. Depending upon the child's age, your expectations should vary as to length and complexity of the content.

OTHER WRITING SUGGESTIONS

Students who want to create a story but don't know what to write can sometimes benefit by the following suggestions. The difficulty levels vary and can be applied to your own situation as needed.

FAVORITE CHARACTERS

Hopefully your students are being introduced to good literature every day in your classroom. If you share books in a series, with the same main characters in each book, and a student seems to enjoy those particular characters, you might suggest that he or she write another story in the series, with a new plot. Kindergartners may enjoy drawing or writing about Mercer Mayer's Little Critter. First- and second-graders might be inspired by characters such as Arnold Lobel's Frog and Toad, Marc Brown's Arthur, or Harry Allard and James Marshall's Miss Nelson. Peggy Parish's Amelia Bedelia might be just the character that inspires third-grade children to write a new story. It is important to remind students that they may base their stories on these characters but that they must write about a new situation that they create. You will want to question the students about their plots to make sure that they are trying to write about a problem and solution of the type that is appropriate for their character.

FAVORITE TYPES OF BOOKS

Third-graders might find more excitement in trying to write a specific type of book. Examples of books they might write in their own version are Fred Gwynne's *A Chocolate Moose for Dinner*, The Magic School Bus series by Joanna Cole and Bruce Degen, or Janet and Allan Ahlberg's *The Jolly Postman*. Each of these titles is

STUART

From *Daily Journals*, published by GoodYearBooks. Copyright © 1993 Carol Simpson.

written in a particular style that the child might want to try to copy in his own words.

FAVORITE AUTHORS

Children who read and listen to good literature often select an author whose books they especially like to read. Although this particular idea is a one-time assignment, it is worth the time it takes to do the task. Suggest that the child write a letter to that favorite author. Some authors take the time to personally answer letters from their fans. What a thrill for the student to have a letter from someone who gives them such pleasure. Suggest that the student tell the author which of his or her books they like best and why, or tell Frank Asch why the little bear in his books would make a good friend. Suggest that Lois Lowry write a story about Anastasia with a plot that is similar to something that happened in the child's own life. Authors get letters like these every day.

POETRY

Children who are introduced to poetry at an early age are excited by the rhythm and rhyme of the verses written with youngsters in mind. If children listen to poetry frequently and are asked to chant along when familiar parts are read, they will soon want to try to write their own rhymes. Build on the child's ability to think of two words that rhyme and then turn those words into a phrase. An example is: a bear in long underwear. Each child in class can create a different rhyming phrase and then illustrate it. Put together a class book of all the rhymes created.

Make the assignment tougher for your second- or third-graders by asking them to write haiku. this type of poem has three lines: the first has five syllables, the second line has seven syllables, and the third has five syllables. For example:

The warm springtime sun
finds shelter in my garden
and makes flowers bloom.

Or have them write two rhyming words such as in *One Sun: A Book of Terse Verse* by Bruce McMillan. Each page has only two words that rhyme, plus an illustration. Examples are "stuck truck" or "lone stone." Polly Cameron's *"I Can't," Said the Ant* is another

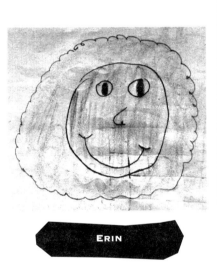

ERIN

From *Daily Journals*, published by GoodYearBooks. Copyright © 1993 Carol Simpson.

approach to poetry. Children who are introduced to poetry and who recite it and hear it read regularly will eventually want to try and write it on their own.

TAKE-OFF STORIES

As the name implies, these stories are based on familiar books that have a repetitive or predictable pattern of events. The easier books such as Bill Martin, Jr.'s *Brown Bear, Brown Bear* can be rewritten in holiday themes, such as "Pumpkin, Pumpkin, What Do You See?"; "Pilgrim, Pilgrim, What Do You See?"; or "Valentine, Valentine, What Do You See?" Seasonal topics with the same idea might include "Snowflake, Snowflake, What Do You See?" or "Robin, Robin, What Do You See?" The topics for take-off books from *Brown Bear, Brown Bear* are limitless!

I Went Walking by Sue Williams offers another pattern that kindergartners and first-graders might enjoy copying in their own words. Children can contribute their own page to a class book of this type of writing as well as a *Brown Bear* take-off story. When you make a class book, be sure you allow the children to check it out overnight to share with parents. They will delight in taking home something they can read to their family, as well as pointing out their own contribution to the project.

Second- and third-graders will find it too simple to copy the very easy pattern stories. They need something with more of a challenge. Books such as *The Important Book* by Margaret Wise Brown require more thought when contributing a page to a class book. Remy Charlip's *Fortunately* offers another interesting pattern for older writers to try to copy. Bernard Most's *If the Dinosaurs Came Back* offers a subject that children delight in sharing.

CIRCLE STORIES

Stories that begin and end in the same place are fun to read. Your older students may enjoy trying to write their own. *If You Give a Mouse a Cookie* by Laura Numeroff is a cute story of this type. *Buzz Buzz Buzz* by Byron Barton is a much easier style to try to copy in one's own words.

Students might work in pairs or small groups to come up with a circle story that contains at least five or six events, each one a consequence of the one before it. Take 6 to 8 pieces of paper and place them in a circle. Begin at the top (12 o'clock position) and

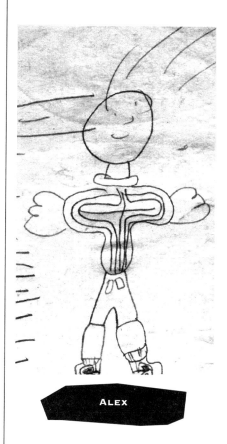

ALEX

write down your beginning and ending point. Then progress around the circle in clockwise order and write down ideas of events that can lead to something else. Try to put your events together in a circle story. Those who succeed in writing a good circle story will find it fun as well as very challenging!

ALEX

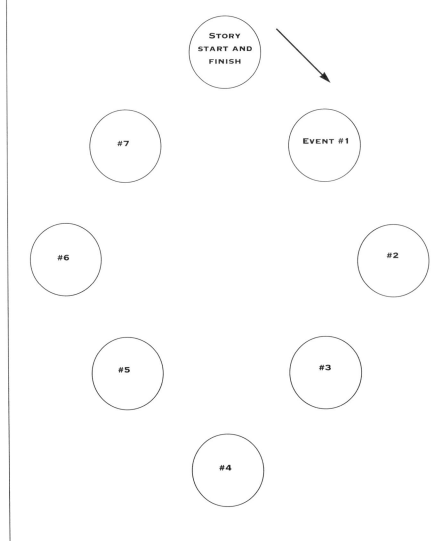

PROGRESSIVE STORIES

These stories have a pattern that repeats itself and builds with each page. Like "The Old Lady Who Swallowed a Fly," these stories begin with a single event and then proceed through a series of events that are remembered page after page. *The Napping House* by Audrey Wood is another good example of a progressive story. This type of story is difficult to write, although somewhat easier than a circle story. Using a story map (see the example on page 26) may be a good way for two or three children to work together and create a progressive story.

PREDICTING A STORY

To do this activity, you will need to select a book that is either brand new or very old—a book that no one has heard or read. The element of surprise is very important here. You will also want your selection to have an involving plot. In addition, the vocabulary in the book needs to lend itself nicely to pulling out interesting phrases or words. Select key phrases and words from the book you've chosen. On the board or on story-starter paper, write the key words and phrases in the order in which they appear in the book. See page 28 for an example of this exercise.

Try not to give away the plot! The students are going to try to guess what happens in the book. You may require that they use all the phrases and words you have given them when they try to write the story the way they think the author has. Have a few of your better writers read their versions of the story before you share the real story.

This is a fun and challenging writing activity; it is probably not useful for kindergarten or first-graders, unless you want to elicit verbal responses to the story instead of written responses.

HOLIDAY GIFT-GIVING

Making a special book for someone as a gift (for birthdays, Christmas, Hanukkah, Mother's Day, Valentine's Day, etc.) is an excellent reason to write a story. The author may want to personalize it to fit the recipient. For example, for Mother's Day the children can write stories about their mothers: What does she do during the day? What special things does she do for you? What would you do if you got to be the mom for a day? Answers to these and

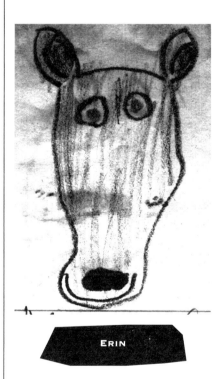

ERIN

From *Daily Journals*, published by GoodYearBooks. Copyright © 1993 Carol Simpson.

Name _____ Date _____

STORY MAP

Title _____

Setting _____

Characters _____

_____

Problem _____

_____

Event #1 _____

_____

Event #2 _____

_____

Event #3 _____

_____

Event #4 _____

_____

Event #5 _____

_____

Solution _____

_____

From Daily Journals, published by GoodYearBooks. Copyright © 1993 Carol Simpson.

other questions make great Mother's Day stories that each child can write, bind, and give as a very special gift.

M.O.T.H.E.R. books are also a good suggestion. An example of a page from this type of book is "M is for macaroni. My mom makes good macaroni." Each letter of the word "mother" is used to tell something special about the child's mom. These books are a sure hit!

A birthday book for someone special (a grandparent) might contain the following completed sentence beginnings: "You are special to me because . . . ." or "The best thing you do for me is . . . ." or "My world would be different without you because . . . ."

WRITING INSTRUCTIONS

Every child, if asked what he or she can make, will come up with an answer. It might be something the child can cook, or it might be an arts and crafts project. Whatever the product, ask the child to write the instructions for performing the task. This is good practice in sequencing. Suggest that they write the steps on separate pieces of paper and then sequence them correctly before writing them into a set of instructions.

NAME ACROSTICS

The child will write each letter of his or her name vertically along the left side of the paper. For each letter, the child needs to think of a word that tells something about himself or herself. Here's an example:

L-lovely

I-intelligent

N-nice

D-dancer

A-artist

The words your children select will reflect their vocabulary understanding beyond just picking words that begin with the right sound. Kindergartners and first-graders might not be ready to try this writing project.

Name _____ Date _____

PREDICTING A STORY

The following words, phrases, and sentences are about a new story that you have not read. It is called *An Alligator Named . . . Alligator* by Lois Grambling. Try to predict what happens in the story by writing it in your own words using the clues in the order that they appear here.

1. Elmo
2. wanted an alligator
3. His sister called him crazy
4. decided not to tell
5. Elmo's father yelled that there was an alligator in the house!!
6. alligator doing laps in his swimming pool
7. zoo
8. waved goodbye
9. two white eggs
10. decided not to tell

From *Daily Journals*, published by GoodYearBooks. Copyright © 1993 Carol Simpson.

STORY STARTERS TO LIGHT THE CREATIVE SPARK

Every now and then it is necessary to give children a story starter and ask everyone in the class to write the rest of the story in his or her own way. The following pages include a number of story-starter pages along with suggestions for introducing each to your students.

If you teach kindergarten or first grade, you might not find as much use for story starters. Kindergarten students are usually not ready to read the sentence that is suppose to spark the story writing. First-grade students may not be ready to complete a story starter until they have written in journals for a couple of months. Halloween or Thanksgiving might be the perfect opportunity to introduce first-graders to the story-starter concept. By then they will have written words and sentences in their journals and will have a better understanding of how to put a story together. Second- and third-grade teachers will find story starters very useful on a regular basis, perhaps twice a month.

You'll find a few examples of actual children's stories throughout this section.

GHOST STORIES

This topic is best suited for Halloween. The idea of the story is obvious. The children are asked to create a ghostly character and then tell a story about how the ghost tried to scare them.

Preparation for writing ghost stories should include a listening-sharing session. Ghost stories need to be read (in a spooky voice, of course) and told. The stories do not have to be long to get a child interested in writing his or her own. The ghost story that Reggie tells Ira in *Ira Sleeps Over* by Bernard Waber is a good example. If you have copies of ghost stories done in the past, it is good to share these because it will give your students an idea of what children of their same age have written.

Have your students sit in a circle. Begin a story and then pass the plot around the circle, each child adding his or her own twists to the story. This kind of brainstorming helps those students who have difficulty creating their own ideas. On a large ghostly shape of white paper, write down the students' responses to "Ghosts are . . . ." This will provide a ready supply of words that might be used in story writing.

Kindergartners and first-graders are usually not ready to write lengthy ghost stories at this time in the year. However, the topic lends itself well to a small "class book" that contains perhaps a dozen stories that have an interesting plot. Allow kindergartners to dictate their stories about the ghostly pictures they have drawn. Then put all pictures with dictated stories together in a big book.

First-graders can write some of the text and with help, they can improve it. Look at the ideas the children have put down on paper and then work with the children who have an interesting plot to develop. It is still early in the year for good stories to come out!

Expect second- and third-graders to write longer stories; again, it may be advantageous to combine stories in a class collection, with everyone contributing, rather than just a select few.

From *Daily Journals*, published by GoodYearBooks. Copyright © 1993 Carol Simpson.

A GHOSTLY TALE

A ghost named _____ tried to scare

me. This is what the ghost did. _____

_____

_____

_____

_____

_____

_____

_____

_____

_____

_____

TRICKY TURKEY

Thanksgiving is an appropriate time to write about how a turkey could trick someone so that he doesn't get eaten for dinner. An introduction of basic information about the foods eaten at the first Thanksgiving might be useful before writing the story. Students might also need to know a little bit about Native Americans and how they lived at that time, including the fact that they hunted for wild turkeys.

Preparation for writing might include a discussion of how the students might trick their friends and family members by hiding somewhere so they do not have to do some task they feel is unpleasant. Lead the discussion to ideas for turkey hiding places and/or turkey tricks.

Kindergarten teachers can allow their students to draw pictures of their tricky turkey and then dictate stories that tell how he escaped the dinner table on Thanksgiving day. Combine the stories in a class book.

First-graders should be able to write at least a few sentences about how the turkey gets away. One illustration might be sufficient to show the main idea. Simple sentences with a definite idea in mind can show a basic understanding of how stories are conceived by their authors. The simple stories can be combined in a class collection; or, if the child has written a lengthy story, it might be suitable for making a cloth book.

Expect second- and third-graders to write longer stories. Those with good strong plots and correct sequencing of events can be bound for sharing with others.

From *Daily Journals*, published by GoodYearBooks. Copyright © 1993 Carol Simpson.

STUART

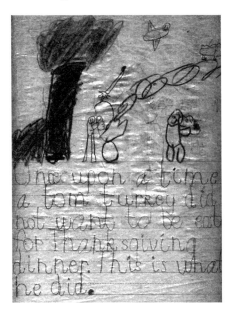

TRICKY TURKEY

A tricky tom turkey did not want to be eaten for Thanksgiving dinner. This is how he kept from being served that day.

_____

_____

_____

_____

_____

HELPING A SICK SANTA

If Santa Claus got sick on Christmas Eve, how would all the toys get delivered to the good boys and girls? What if Santa came to your house, got sick, and asked you to help him finish his work?

Preparation for writing might include a discussion about how you feel when you get sick. Then ask: How does Santa deliver the toys? Do you think you could fly with Santa and Rudolph? Could you slide down chimneys just like Santa? Talk about the story being "fiction" and not "fact" to allow the children the freedom to let their imaginations fly.

This topic is especially fun for kindergartners and first-graders to write because they are (usually) believers in Santa. Second- and third-graders might be more difficult to inspire with this topic.

From *Daily Journals*, published by GoodYearBooks. Copyright © 1993 Carol Simpson.

TROUBLE AT CHRISTMAS

Santa was sick when he came down my chimney.

He asked me to help deliver all the presents.

So I did. _____

_____

_____

_____

_____

_____

_____

DECEMBER DECORATING

Because some students do not celebrate Christmas, but DO have a December celebration, this story starter is good for any traditions that require decorating for the month.

Preparation for this writing project should include a discussion of how families decorate, what they hang in their homes, what their traditions are, etc. This might even lead to a study of winter celebrations around the world. Perhaps school families with various backgrounds would come in and share their family traditions that go back for generations. Children need to be aware that people around the world celebrate in different ways.

From *Daily Journals*, published by GoodYearBooks. Copyright © 1993 Carol Simpson.

DECEMBER DECORATING

December is a fun month because we decorate

the house for _____. This is

what we do _____

_____

_____

_____

_____

_____

_____

_____

MAGIC SNOWPEOPLE

In many parts of the world, winter time means snow. Students of all primary grades can't wait to build their first snowman when they see that the ground is white. They also get excited about making snow forts, snow angels, and having snowball fights.

Stir the imagination just a bit with this story starter. Remind your kindergartners and first-graders about Frosty the Snowman, and that he became magic when a hat was placed upon his head. Have the children brainstorm other items that you place somewhere on a snowperson (lumps of coal for eyes, a carrot nose, perhaps a scarf, or sticks for arms). What would happen if one of these things made your snowperson magic? What would your magic snowperson do? On a large shape paper, brainstorm their reactions to the phrase "Magic snowpeople could . . . ." This will provide additional vocabulary. After the discussion, allow your students time to draw and write their stories.

Second- and third-graders might enjoy creating an adventure that the magic snowperson has when he or she (1) visits school, (2) gets lost on a busy street corner, (3) starts melting on a sunny day, or (4) doesn't want to go away when spring arrives.

From *Daily Journals*, published by GoodYearBooks. Copyright © 1993 Carol Simpson.

MY MAGIC
SNOWPERSON

One winter day I went outside

and built a person made of snow.

It became a magic snowperson when I

placed a _____ on it. This is

what happened. _____

_____

_____

_____

_____

_____

LEPRECHAUNS

March wouldn't be complete without some talk about St. Patrick's Day and leprechauns. Even kindergartners have heard of the tricky little creatures. They know about the pots of gold leprechauns have hidden at the end of the rainbow. Children enjoy pretending such things do exist.

To prepare for writing/drawing, ask the students how they would catch a leprechaun. Brainstorm endings to the following phrase: "Leprechauns are . . . ." Put the responses on the board so students can use the words in stories that tell how they catch a leprechaun and what they would do with a pot of gold. Students of all primary grades love to fantasize about having a lot of money to spend. This story is appropriate for K-3, with teachers of each grade level having their own expectations for length and complexity of the resulting stories.

From *Daily Journals*, published by GoodYearBooks. Copyright © 1993 Carol Simpson.

LEPRECHAUNS

A leprechaun named _____

has a pot of gold. This is how I plan to get it.

_____

_____

_____

_____

_____

_____

_____

_____

EASTER BUNNY HELPERS

The tradition of coloring and giving Easter eggs in baskets extends beyond kindergarten and first grade, even if the belief in the Easter Bunny does not. Five- to seven-year-olds will delight in imagining that the Easter Bunny came to ask for their help in painting and distributing all the eggs. The story lends itself nicely to an egg shape. Collect class stories and bind them in an egg-shaped book.

Tell your third-graders that they are going to write Easter Bunny stories to share with the kindergarten and first-grade classes. Remind them before writing that the belief in the Easter Bunny is still strong in their audience. Allow students the opportunity to visit the younger classes and share their stories in small groups. This activity is especially beneficial for third-graders who are poorer readers/writers because their stories will be accepted by their young audience. It gives them a chance to sound like a good reader and story writer.

Turn the assignment into a math lesson for your second- or third-graders. How many eggs does the Easter Bunny need if every student in class is going to receive 5 eggs? Or, how many eggs are needed for your entire school population? What if the children in grades K, 1, and 2 get 6 eggs each and 3, 4, and 5 get 10 eggs each? The possibilities are endless for creating math problems of varying difficulty for all of your students.

From *Daily Journals*, published by GoodYearBooks. Copyright © 1993 Carol Simpson.

EASTER BUNNY HELPERS

The Easter Bunny asked me to

help paint and deliver eggs because

_____

_____

_____

_____

_____

_____

_____

_____

RAINY-DAY STORIES

Are you willing to admit that you wish you were a kid and could go splashing when you see a big puddle outside? Children have a natural love of jumping in and splashing around. Mom can say "no" over and over again, but it doesn't sink in. Kids love splashing and getting wet!

For most children, the story they write for this assignment will not be fiction. Most will write about a real experience they have had with a big puddle. Most of their moms said, "Don't get wet!" and the words just went in one ear and out the other. Kids of all ages can create this story. They love to share their experiences with their peers, if only to see who has the wettest tale to tell.

Your cover for this story might well be a window pane with raindrops running down; perhaps with a rainbow showing outside. Open your windowpane cover in the center to expose the story inside.

From *Daily Journals*, published by GoodYearBooks. Copyright © 1993 Carol Simpson.

One rainy day...

MY RAINY DAY STORY

One rainy day in April I found a big puddle. Mom said, "Don't get wet!", but I sure had fun anyway! _____

_____

_____

_____

_____

_____

_____

SUMMER VACATION

Many teachers have started the school year by asking their new students to write about their summer vacations. This writing activity provides the teacher with samples of the new students' varied abilities to use written language. Instead of writing about vacation at the beginning of the year, why not use this story starter near the end of the school year, just before summer vacation begins? Families begin to make summer plans and the children begin to anticipate visiting new places, seeing grandparents, riding the rides at their favorite theme parks, and other summertime fun.

Preparation for this writing activity might include a discussion of trips the family is planning, sports the students plan to play, or their favorite thing about summer. Second- and third-graders might look at travel brochures for vacation destinations, and even create some of their own brochures for real or pretend places they would like to visit.

If your school allows field trips, visit the local public library to find out about summer reading programs. If you can't take a field trip, make some lemonade and drink it while sitting outside under a big tree on a warm day in late May. Talk about summer vacation plans as you relax. Even children who don't plan to travel or participate in sports will enjoy writing about what they do to have fun on a hot summer day.

From *Daily Journals*, published by GoodYearBooks. Copyright © 1993 Carol Simpson.

SUMMER VACATION

My summer vacation will be fun. This is what I plan to do. _____

END-OF-THE-YEAR LETTERS

At or near the end of the year, tell your students that they are now "experts" about what goes on in their current grade level. Remind them of just how nervous they were when they began the school year some nine months ago. Wouldn't they have felt more comfortable about entering a new room if someone would have warned them or prepared them for what was ahead?

The idea of this story starter is to have your children write to next year's class and tell them about your room. Your students will want to tell what they like best, what they like least, how hard (or easy) they think the work is, and whether or not you are a nice teacher. After the letters are written, share them with the appropriate grade level teachers so that their children can hear some of the things your students want to tell them in preparation for going on to the next grade. Kindergarten teachers, instead of warning next year's class, might ask your students to write or draw what they like best about the year in your room.

Dear First grade,
It is fun in 2nd grade. I saw some new things on the first day of school. Every Friday some body gets an apple A real one too. There are two jars, and one of them has 100 marbles. The other one you have to earn the marble to get Extra recess and other good stuff. But you can only get those things in Mrs. Clarks class. She has her own homeroom, computer and typewriter. There will be some jobs. You will have an apple with a piece of paper on it, that says your name on it. You will have story time, and you will get to hold an animal and somebody gets to sit in the story chair. At silent reading she will give out passes so people can sit at her desk.
Sinserly,
Mary Pank...

DEAR KINDERGARTNERS,

This is what I would like to tell you about the first grade. _____

_____

_____

_____

_____

_____

_____

_____

_____

CRAYONS

A

DEAR FIRST- GRADERS,

There is a lot going on in the second grade! This is what I want to tell you about it so you will be ready.

THE FIRST READER

1

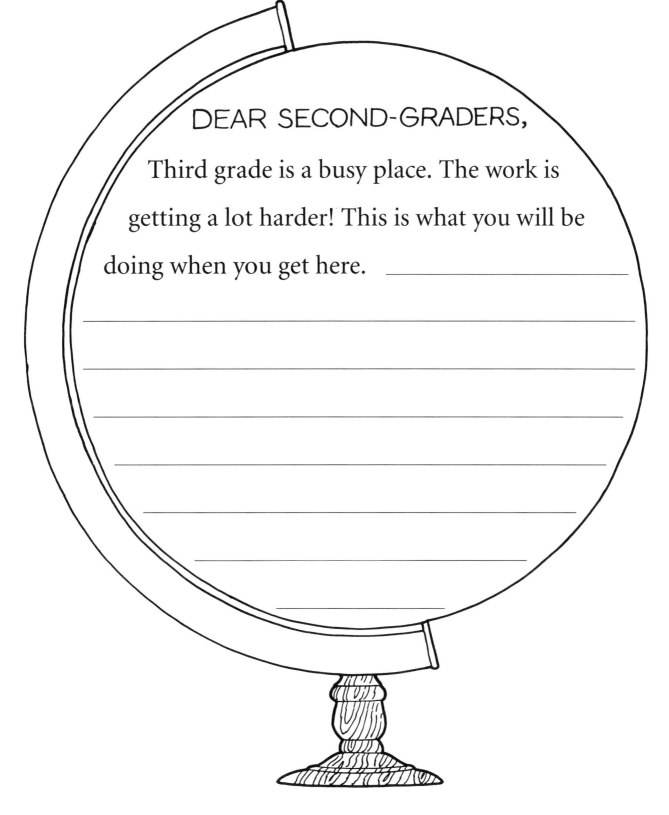

DEAR SECOND-GRADERS,

Third grade is a busy place. The work is getting a lot harder! This is what you will be doing when you get here. _____

_____

_____

_____

_____

_____

_____

"Owie" Stories

Ask your children to draw a large (*large* is the key here) picture of themselves on a sheet of 18" x 24" drawing paper the "tall way." Tell them that they must not put a smile on their face just yet. They may not want to be smiling when they finish with this project. Set the pictures aside, to be finished later.

Have the children talk about their "owies," different scrapes and scratches that they have gotten. How did they get them? Did they ever require stitches? You will hear stories all the way from bicycle accidents, to dog bites, to fights with siblings, to jumping through a glass table (yes, this one is true!), to things you couldn't imagine. All will come to life in the stories the children will tell and then write.

Finally, the last step is to give each child a bandage to place somewhere on the large picture they have drawn. Write about the "owie" that is underneath the bandage and how they got it.

There is no single time of year for this writing project, and no age limit for inspiring creativity. Children in kindergarten through third grade delight in telling of their mishaps. Most are true; some are fiction based on fact; some are wild stretches of the imagination. Be prepared for lots of fun!

From *Daily Journals*, published by GoodYearBooks. Copyright © 1993 Carol Simpson.

AN "OWIE" STORY

I got an "owie." It hurt! this is what happened. _____

TEDDY BEARS

Many youngsters go to sleep every night with a favorite stuffed toy—not just teddy bears. This story could be about any stuffed animal that the child might wish were real. Perhaps you will want to adapt this story starter to your needs by allowing the children to line out "teddy bears" and write their own animal choice in its place.

Preparation for writing this story needs to include a discussion about stuffed animals and how the students feel about theirs. The children may want to bring their favorite animal to school to show when their story is ready for sharing. Classmates can see the actual subject of the story and find out about the animal, similar to a show and tell time.

Because many children talk to their stuffed animals, it should be easy for them to imagine what would happen if they came to life. Where would you take your stuffed animal? What games would you play together? Would you tell your friends about it or keep it a secret? How could it happen that the animal came to life? These and other questions would help the children write their stories.

My Magic Teddybear   2-7-92
by
Erin

My teddybear came to life!
Imagine that! We had such fun.
This is what we did. we played
with the other teddybears
we had lots of fun that
we jumped, we ran, we jumped
up and down my mother called
"Erin! time to eat!" we went
to bed. I asked mom
If I cold have dinner
with my teddybear. she
said, "it will ok" The teddy
bear and I Went down
stairs in the basment
I had dinner and tea.

ERIN

MY TEDDY BEAR STORY

My teddy bear came to life! Imagine that! We had

such fun. This is what we did.

PETS

Children who do not have pets always seem to wish they had a dog or a cat. It is one of the joys of childhood, growing and learning about animals by taking care of one. In the book *All About Sam* by Lois Lowry, a worm becomes Sam's pet since Sam's dad is allergic to animal fur. Children can justify all kinds of creatures as being good pets for a myriad of reasons. Fish don't bark or leave messes on the floor; dogs help guard the house against intruders; cats will catch mice; spiders are friendly and they eat bugs.

For this story, children have no limits when writing about the ideal pet. Through brainstorming, children can get ideas for some unusual pets they would like to have, and why they would be good pets. Some may write about a pet they really have, others will write about a pet they would like to have.

From *Daily Journals*, published by GoodYearBooks. Copyright © 1993 Carol Simpson.

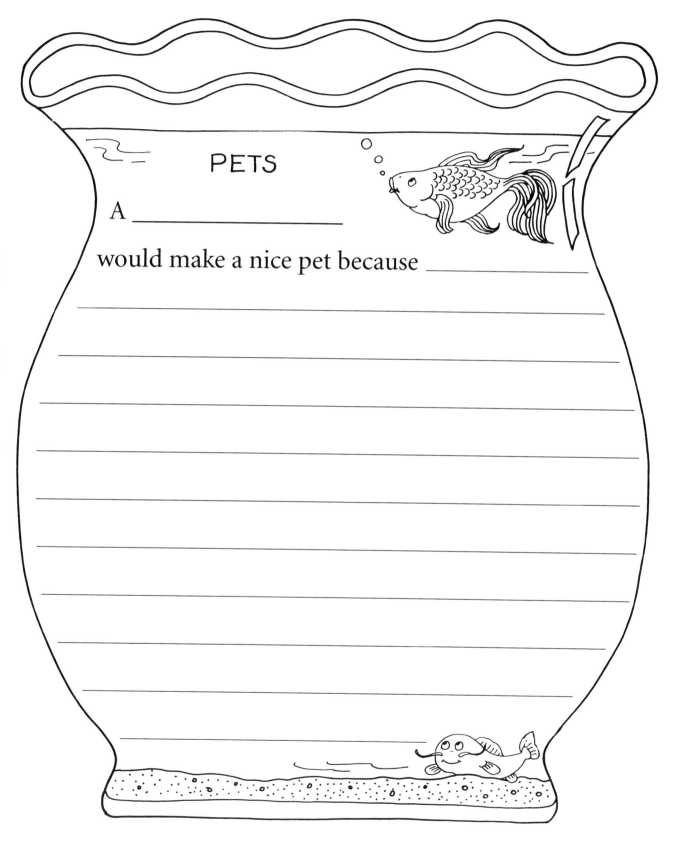

PETS

A _____

would make a nice pet because _____

_____

_____

_____

_____

_____

_____

_____

_____

_____

DINOSAURS

Students of all ages love to read and learn about the dinosaurs. Their size, their fierceness, and their mystery seem to draw kids to them. Many children's books have been written on the theme of these huge animals coming to life today and playing with children. They stir the imagination.

Children need to hear some of their favorite dinosaur stories to get them interested in examining the possibility of life with dinosaurs today. They can come up with great ideas about how dinosaurs could help us in numerous ways.

Preparation for this writing assignment might include (besides hearing books on the subject) brainstorming about jobs that we wish we didn't have to do. Are there some jobs that dinosaurs could do for us? Would they be useful as a means of transportation? Would they replace machines such as cranes? Could they help around the house? Where would they live? What would you feed them? Once your students have discussed these and other questions on the subject, they will be ready to write.

In the story below, notice how Alex writes about dinosaurs and demonstrates an attempt to use the silent *e* rule in the words "theye," "mace," and "slizse."

From *Daily Journals*, published by GoodYearBooks. Copyright © 1993 Carol Simpson.

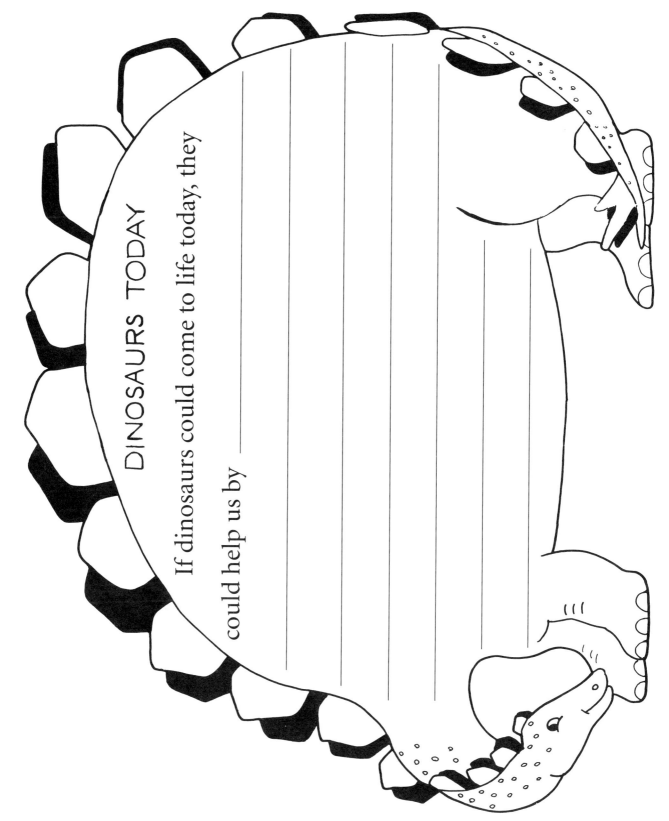

DINOSAURS TODAY

If dinosaurs could come to life today, they

could help us by _____

GREEN ME

Prepare the children for this story starter by asking the following questions: What's it like to wake up in the morning and find out that you have measles? How do you look? How do you feel? What if you woke up and found out that your hair had changed color in the night? How could it have happened? How would you deal with it? What if you woke up in the morning and your whole body had turned green? How could it happen? Could eating something make you turn green? Could you have been hit by a can of green paint? And once you determine how it happened, what will you do about it? Will it wash off? Is it a permanent change? What will your friends think when they see you? Now write a story about it.

From *Daily Journals*, published by GoodYearBooks. Copyright © 1993 Carol Simpson.

GREEN ME

I woke up this morning and found that

I was all green! _____

_____

_____

_____

_____

_____

_____

_____

_____

_____

_____

SURPRISES

Children of all ages can write a story about the best surprise they ever had. Every child has gotten something they didn't expect or been taken somewhere and not told where he or she was going so that it would be a surprise.

Brainstorm the phrase "Surprises are . . . ." This will give your students words and ideas that they might use in their own stories. Have several children talk about surprises that have taken place in their own lives. By hearing others' stories, those who have a more difficult time getting ideas will perhaps be reminded of something similar that happened to them. Your students should not copy someone else's story, but each might be able to write about his or her own event after hearing what others share.

SURPRISE !

I just love surprises! You never know what to expect. I will never forget when I got a really big surprise! This is what happened. _____

_____

_____

_____

_____

_____

_____

_____

_____

MY FAVORITE TRIP

Most children have taken a special trip at some time, whether it be 50 miles or 2,000 miles away from their own town. Perhaps they went to visit Grandma; perhaps they went to a theme park and got to ride the rides; perhaps they went on an airplane for the first time; perhaps they went out of the country.

List on the board or a sheet of poster-sized paper some of the places your students say they have visited. Include a social studies lesson by locating the places on a map and marking these with pins. Some may have visited the same places. Even though two students write about the same vacation spot, they will write different stories because their experiences will not have been exactly the same.

Ask students to write about what they did while they were on the trip, what they liked the best, and what they disliked about the place. They can write about a typical day at this vacation spot, beginning with getting up and ending with going to bed. You might even ask your students to write what happened by the hour, much like keeping a travel log. If a student has not taken a favorite trip, he or she can write about a place he or she hopes to be able to visit some day.

Other ideas include writing a travel brochure for a favorite vacation place. A student may make a tri-fold pamphlet that has pictures (drawn or taken from magazines or travel ads) and narrative about the highlights of the place. Ask the child to think of how he or she would "sell" a favorite place to someone who has never been there.

From *Daily Journals*, published by GoodYearBooks. Copyright © 1993 Carol Simpson.

MY FAVORITE TRIP

Did you miss me? I've been gone! I just went on the greatest trip ever. I went to _____

PERSONIFICATION: ANIMAL

Ask the children to pretend they are animals: What animal would you like to be, and why? Talk about different kinds of animals. List or graph animals by characteristics. Some are furry, some are not. Some are fierce, some are not. Some live on land, some on water. Some animals are wild, some can be tamed. Some animals are large, some are small. Children should select one that they like. It might be best if you require that each child pretend to be a different animal.

Once children select their animals, they will want to find more information: what it eats; where it lives; the sound it makes—if any; very special characteristics it has that make it different from other animals, and any other information that might be important in writing about themselves as that animal.

Depending upon the amount of research your students can do, you can expect some detailed stories about how each child spends his or her day as that animal. While kindergartners may only draw a picture and dictate a sentence or two about their animal, first-graders might write about why they would want to be that animal. Second- or third-graders can get more detailed about where they would live and what they would eat and how they would spend a day as a particular animal.

From *Daily Journals*, published by GoodYearBooks. Copyright © 1993 Carol Simpson.

I'M AN ANIMAL !

If I could be any animal in the world, I would like

to be a _____ because

_____

_____

_____

_____

PERSONIFICATION: PERSON

As with the previous story idea, the student will put himself or herself in someone else's shoes. Depending upon the ability of your students to do research on another person (by interviewing someone, or studying a famous person in a historical biography), the requirements will vary.

Kindergartners might want to be you, a parent, or their best friend. A picture and sentence, "I would like to be _____ because . . ." might be all you can expect. At the opposite end is the story that the older student writes after interviewing the principal, the school nurse, a teacher, or other person they would like to be. Challenge your gifted students to first read about a historical figure they might like to be and then write their personification story.

From *Daily Journals*, published by GoodYearBooks. Copyright © 1993 Carol Simpson.

THE NEW ME

I wish I could go to sleep and wake up as someone else. If I could be any person in the world, I would like to be _____ because

_____

_____

_____

_____

_____

_____

_____

GIVING SOMETHING SPECIAL

This writing activity is more appropriate for older students. Begin by asking your students if they have a special possession that they cherish. It might be an old coin that their grandfather gave to them, it might be a special locket or other piece of jewelry that has been passed down in their family. Or maybe it is a special rock that they found while taking a walk with their dog. It does not matter what the item is, nor how they got it; the important thing to keep in mind is that it is to be something very special in their lives.

Ask each child to think about becoming an old person who wants to give away the special something. Ask the children to think about who the recipient might be and why. How would you go about telling that person just how special the object is? How can you be sure they will treat it with special care?

From *Daily Journals*, published by GoodYearBooks. Copyright © 1993 Carol Simpson.

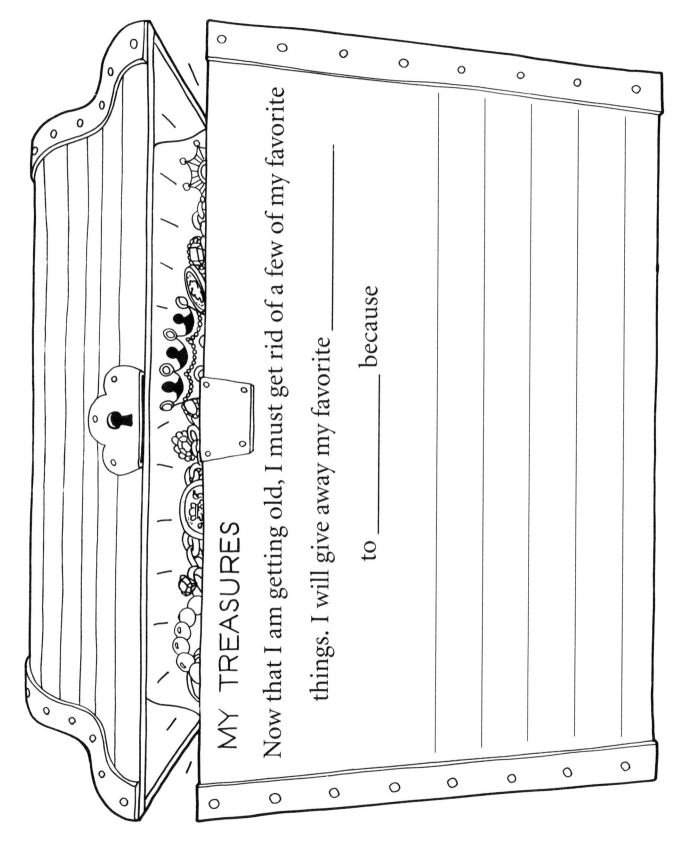

MY TREASURES

Now that I am getting old, I must get rid of a few of my favorite things. I will give away my favorite _____ to _____ because

THREE WISHES

Everyone makes wishes! Grown-ups and children alike wish they had something they don't have right now. Talk about the children's wishes. Ask them what they would do if they won the lottery. They always have ideas! They know what they would buy.

This story is a slight twist on winning the lottery. It is a good writing assignment after hearing the book *Wriggles, The Little Wishing Pig* by Pauline Watson or *The Three Wishes* by Charles Perrault.

Ask the children what they might wish for if someone granted them the opportunity to get whatever they wanted. Then have the children write their own stories of what they would wish for if a tree fairy granted them three wishes.

THREE WISHES

Once upon a time, a tree fairy granted me three wishes. I

thought and thought! What could I wish? I finally decided.

Here is what I wished. _____

BOOKWORMS

Begin this story-starter exercise by discussing some of these questions with the class:

What is a bookworm? Of course, it is someone who enjoys reading books! Are you a bookworm? Do you enjoy reading? What kinds of books do you like to read? Do you have a favorite book?

How did you become a bookworm? When do you think it happened? Did someone read to you or give you a book that became one of your favorites?

Think about being a bookworm. Write a story that tells how and when you became a bookworm. Tell what happened to turn you on to books. Write about your favorite book or author.

After discussing these suggested questions, give students the bookworm story-starters. When the children are finished, combine the stories into an accordion bookworm by mounting them on heavy manila paper or posterboard circles. See page 12 for an example. Add the head and tail, and display the bookworms on a long shelf or table.

From *Daily Journals*, published by GoodYearBooks. Copyright © 1993 Carol Simpson.

LUCKY ME!
I'M A BOOKWORM!

EVALUATION ISSUES

SPELLING

INVENTED SPELLING

It is sad to see many young authors who begin a story with a good idea and then are stifled because they don't know how to spell all of the words they want to write. They have been encouraged by teachers and parents to spell correctly whenever they write something. Spelling *is* important! But when doing creative writing, spelling should be a secondary concern for the student. The first consideration is the plot or the idea of the story. The ideas that are in the child's head need to be put down on paper. They will be forgotten if the child expects perfection!

Children need to be allowed the freedom to invent spelling so that they get their stories written. As the name implies, invented spelling is a child's way of writing down words he or she cannot spell perfectly without asking the teacher for help or looking in a dictionary.

It takes time to develop independence and confidence in a child's ability to put down "words" that someone can read, even though they are spelled wrong. Students who have been taught to invent their spelling from the beginning, in kindergarten and first grade, will usually take pencil in hand and begin writing. They do not let spelling problems get in the way of their stories. Those students who have not been allowed to invent their words are more than likely going to ask the teacher how to spell a large portion of the words in their stories. They need to come to the realization that correct spelling is nice, but it is not the purpose of the writing experience.

ERIN

Neither is a neat and tidy paper! Children who fear turning in a less than perfect-looking paper need to be reassured that it is all right to make mistakes. They need to know that someone else will probably be able to read their story if they write down the letters they think they hear in a word. Your parents may need to be re-educated into accepting this philosophy. If you take the time to explain invented spelling to them, as well as show them examples of the stages of development that their children will exhibit, they will be more willing to give it a chance. The results will become more obvious to them as the year progresses.

Reading invented spelling becomes easier with practice. When you begin, it is a good idea to ask the author to read the story to you. Take note of a child's ability to use correct consonants at the beginnings and endings of the words being read to you. Vowels are usually the last letters to be used correctly. In fact, in early invented spelling, vowels are often completely forgotten! After some practice, invented spelling is really not difficult to decode. Once in a while you will have to ask a child what a word might be. If it is tough to decode, you might try to jot down notes to yourself about the basic idea of the story so that the next time the child comes to see you about the story you can say, "Oh, yes. This story is about . . . ." You might be surprised at the smiles you get when the child thinks you really *can* read the story!

THE STAGES OF INVENTED SPELLING

Invented spelling develops in stages, and the first stage is scribbling. (See the Appendix for examples of this and most other stages of invented spelling.) In this stage, the child picks up a pencil or crayon and makes marks on the paper. Ask the child what it says, and he or she will tell you a story. A few scribbles can lead to a very long tale! The child is copying the process that he or she has observed in grown-ups. Because children want to feel grown up, they will copy what they think is adult behavior. If they see adults writing grocery lists or letters to Grandma, children will try to copy the behavior by writing their own lists and letters. The adult model is very important to the child.

By the time a child gets to school, scribbling changes to a process of writing down letters of the alphabet. Often you will see unusual letter combinations that the child will "read" as a story or a note to someone.

MARY

From *Daily Journals*, published by GoodYearBooks. Copyright © 1993 Carol Simpson.

This second stage of invented spelling is just as difficult to read as is the scribbling in the earlier stage, because the selected letters often have no relationship to what the child tells you it is meant to say. Kindergarten teachers have the most difficult job when it comes to reading invented spelling. Gradually there is purpose to the letters being put down on the paper because the children begin to learn to listen for, and write down, beginning sounds of words.

In the next stage of invented spelling the child begins to write more than just the initial consonant of a word. Instead of one letter, you will see at least two and sometimes more. The child is listening more carefully and trying to pick up more of the consonants heard. The invented spelling is becoming somewhat easier to read. If you ask the child to "read" the story to you, he or she will do it; and will do it again the next day in exactly the same words even though you might have thought that the garbled letter combinations couldn't say anything!

Then there is the child who wants the teacher to read her journal. If the teacher cannot read the words, the child thinks she hasn't really written anything. This child needs a pep talk that includes some encouraging words: "Your journal says whatever you say it says!" Just because the teacher can't read it does not mean that it has no meaning. This child needs praise for trying to write words—even though it is difficult to read what they say. If she continues to feel that her work has no meaning, she will be discouraged about writing for some time. First-graders are especially sensitive about their ability to write what someone can read.

Vowels begin to appear in writing once a child has been introduced to the idea that words are suppose to contain at least one of them. Vowel sounds are difficult for youngsters to hear and are often incorrectly used in invented spelling. Once a child begins to understand that there are rules that make the vowels long or short, you will see their attempts at showing long vowels, often by adding a silent *e* at the end of a word. Children will show you how much they are learning in their reading by trying to use new skills in their writing. As children progress in their understanding of phonics and how letters work together to make sounds, their spelling gets increasingly better. By no means should we think that spelling will be perfect before children leave primary

From *Daily Journals*, published by GoodYearBooks. Copyright © 1993 Carol Simpson.

MARY

grades; but we should see gradual improvement, which, along with dictionary skills, should lead to fewer spelling errors.

PERSONAL DICTIONARIES

Some teachers feel that students will not produce finished writing samples unless they can spell most of their words correctly. However, children cannot be allowed to ask for a teacher's help in spelling every single word they want to write.

If you are one of these teachers, try using personal dictionaries in your class. A personal dictionary is a simple booklet—made by stapling together blank sheets of paper—which contains one page for each letter of the alphabet. (Blank journals purchased from teacher supply catalogs also work well.) Each child keeps a personal dictionary at his or her desk or workspace. The dictionary contains the words that that child needs when writing stories.

Personal dictionaries are used for special words, words that the children could not spell on their own. These are often words with two or more syllables. When introducing a writing assignment to the class, hold a brainstorming session to generate a list of words that might be used for the assignment. Write the words on the board so that students can copy them into the dictionaries. This will save your having to spell the same words over and over as children want to use them later.

If you teach first or second grade, you may be asked to write the words in the students' dictionaries. Third-graders should be expected to try to find a word in a published dictionary before writing it in a personal dictionary.

MARKING STUDENT JOURNALS

Opinions differ on the subject of how much marking teachers should be doing in students' journals. On the one hand there are those who feel that journals should be marked to show the writer where there are errors in using punctuation marks, or words that are spelled incorrectly. Those teachers who have this opinion feel that the students' writing skills will improve if mistakes are plainly marked.

Some kindergarten and first-grade teachers share the opinion that mistakes should be marked. These teachers want

MARY

From *Daily Journals*, published by GoodYearBooks. Copyright © 1993 Carol Simpson.

parents to be able to read what is written in journals that come home with the children. If children are writing in early stages of invented spelling, parents may not be able to read the stories unless they are recopied or corrected before going home. By correcting the mistakes, the teacher is allowing the parent to read the story at home.

On the other side of the issue are those teachers who would never write or mark in a student's journal because it is too discouraging for the young authors to see so many red marks on their work. Students are proud of their effort when they think they have written something interesting, something that others would enjoy hearing. Teachers who do not believe in marking journals think that making corrections diminishes the child's pride in accomplishment.

When students take home their journals for sharing with families, they want to read the words. They don't want mom or dad to read it to themselves later, perhaps after the child goes to bed. Children want the pat on the back that they get when they read a story they wrote all by themselves. If parents can read the story without the child's help—and stories that have been red-lined and corrected do not require assistance from the child—the child misses out on that pat on the back.

You need to determine which philosophy you wish to follow. If you decide to mark journals, then mark them all with equal gusto. Do not be concerned that stories are full of red marks! If you decide that you will never mark a journal, stick to your decision. Never mark a journal, even though you see things that you would love to correct before the journal goes home for mom and dad to see. Children who invent their spelling and do not correct it before taking a journal home often have some words spelled in ways that would raise a few eyebrows! (See the Appendix for a few examples.)

MARY

CHECKING STUDENT PROGRESS

Assessing progress is not difficult if you keep an assortment of the children's written work to review periodically. What you will be looking for will vary with the grade level you teach.

If you teach kindergarten, you will be assessing the children's ability to progress from scribble-writing or unusual letter

combinations to attempts at writing words and phrases that seem to have some meaning.

First-grade teachers can examine the progress children make in their ability to invent more appropriate spelling of the words they want to write. Watch for changes in the amount of writing being done on the journal pages or the space filled with quality writing on story starters. At the beginning of the year, students will write single words or two- and three-word phrases. By year's end they should be writing several sentences on a journal page; they should be able to fill the lines on a story starter with appropriate text. At this age children should not be expected to make great improvements in their ability to spell all or most of their words correctly. Be ready to read journals filled with misspelled words (unless these are the words that the children asked to have written in the personal dictionaries). Even words that appear on weekly spelling tests are often misspelled in daily journal writing!

Teachers in the second grade should be looking for continued progress in spelling words correctly. At this stage, students should also begin to have a basic understanding of the use of punctuation marks and capital letters. The children's writing should begin to show how much they understand by the way they put in periods and capital letters in sometimes inappropriate places. If you choose to make marks in journals, be prepared to put in most capital letters and periods. Even though they have an understanding of how punctuation is used, children are not ready to use this skill accurately. However, look for some improvement.

Third-grade teachers can expect to see the least amount of mistakes in written language. Although the work will not be perfect, the children should be able to use most capital letters and punctuation marks correctly. If capitals and punctuation are incorrect, the child should try reading the story aloud and will perhaps catch some of his or her mistakes. Look for continued improvement in writing more complex sentences with correct adjectives and adverbs. Stories should become longer, with a series of events that show good sequencing ability.

If you keep a selection of stories and journals to show to parents at conference time, they will also be able to see a child's progress.

From *Daily Journals*, published by GoodYearBooks. Copyright © 1993 Carol Simpson.

THE FINISHED PRODUCT

Children will take more interest in writing stories if they know that other people are going to read what they write. There is value in writing stories if they will be shared, not just filed away.

Before presenting their writing to a reader, children need to learn that they must re-write a "sloppy copy" using proper spelling and language so that others can read and understand what is written. This process of writing, editing, and presenting the finished product is a rewarding exercise in learning to use language effectively.

CONFERENCING WITH STUDENTS

Every child, regardless of age, needs to be given one-on-one time with the teacher for the purpose of reading (telling) the stories in their journals. They need to have the positive feedback from the teacher. They need to be told that their story is good, that "all you have to do is. . ." to make it a bit more interesting. They want to know if their story is good enough to bind with a cover.

Scheduling a conference time with each child on a regular basis is up to you. Some children want to show how they are making progress every day; others only show their finished story; still others come around only when they get stuck and can't think of anything to write. As a rule, children will visit the teacher when they think they need to!

When you are "in conference" with a writer, it is important that the others know that they should not interrupt the conversation. Make a "Do Not Disturb" sign that you can put up somewhere whenever you are in conference. Even kindergartners can be taught to honor the sign.

MARY

An important conferencing time is when you and a child are editing a story. Even the youngest students need to realize that the stories they write need editing. They are not ready for an audience until the spelling and language are in proper form. Children often copy adult behavior; and they need to copy adult behavior by writing their stories the way grown-ups do, using correct spelling and language.

KINDERGARTEN

Kindergarten teachers do not need to worry about their children doing any of the editing of their writing. If a kindergartner should happen to write a story worth turning into a bound book of one kind or another, the teacher will have to do all editing: Correcting the spelling and putting in the appropriate capital letters and punctuation marks before a story is typed in finished form. It is important that you remember to leave incorrect verb tenses as they are written (or dictated). When the child shares the story, he or she will read the incorrect verb tenses as they were before editing. If the child says "runned" when reading/telling the story, this is the way it needs to appear in edited form as well. If you change the word sequence in any way, the child will notice. Whenever possible, it adds to the child's dictated story if you will attempt to spell some of the words the way the children pronounce them. An example of this is "pisgetti" rather than spaghetti, if they are dictating recipes or favorite foods.

FIRST GRADE

If you teach first grade, do not expect much in the way of editing on the part of your students either. When you sit down with the child for a final conference, point out where capital letters and punctuation marks are needed as *you* copy the story on a separate sheet of paper. Remember *not* to change the verb tense in incorrectly written sentences because the child will notice the changes you make. Point out where there are run-on sentences that need to be shortened. Show him or her how to do it and let the child read and understand why you take out the "and" when it appears too often. Explain that by taking out the "and" you can start a new sentence on a new page, thus making a longer story for a bound book.

ALEX

From *Daily Journals*, published by GoodYearBooks. Copyright © 1993 Carol Simpson.

First-graders are not yet ready to try to interpret editing marks and copy their own stories. The only copy they write is their "sloppy copy." If you give the child writing lines in a cloth book, then he or she can copy the story in final form. But be prepared to find errors in the copying that is done by the student authors at this age. Try putting the appropriate words for each page on sticky notes. As the child puts the edited work on the proper page, he or she can throw away the sticky note. Copying the correct words on the page is easier this way than it is for the child to see the edited story on a single sheet of paper, and then try to figure out which sentences belong together on which page. When possible, type the words to the story in appropriate spacing so that the sentences or paragraphs could be cut and glued in their proper place in a bound book. The children really like the looks of a typed story, rather than their own handwritten pages.

The typical editing session with a first-grader might include the following steps:

1.   The child reads the story aloud.

2.   Talk with the child about the topic of the story and whether it is maintained throughout the story; if something does not fit the topic, talk about why, and perhaps eliminate the inappropriate parts with the child's permission.

3.   Look at spelling errors with the child. As you copy the story on a separate sheet of paper, write the corrected spelling and show the child. Point out words that have been on any spelling lists and should have been spelled correctly. Also point out words for which the child did an excellent job of inventing spellings.

4.   When recopying on separate paper, point out, and correct, places where students have left out capital letters (and why they are needed) as well as punctuation marks (and an explanation of their use).

SECOND AND THIRD GRADE

Second- and third-graders are old enough to begin to do some of their own editing. Don't expect perfection. The capitalization and punctuation skills that have been introduced and taught for sever-

ERIN

BRANDON

al years may still not be a normal part of the child's writing. Teachers can show their students some simple editing marks that indicate misspelled words to correct, punctuation marks that are missing, or capital letters that were omitted. The children can copy their "sloppy copy" and try to improve their errors.

Third-graders are more apt to find each other's mistakes in writing than to spot their own errors. Let your third-graders pair up with a buddy to do some editing of each other's work before you see their stories. Often by reading aloud to a buddy, the student will notice run-on sentences or incorrect verb tenses. The writers usually know which words they might have misspelled and which words they are certain are correct. Capital letters and punctuation marks might be spotted best when a buddy reads the story.

The editing conference steps on page 85 are also appropriate for second and third grade editing conferences. However, you should expect to have to point out fewer and fewer of the child's errors.

As students become better writers, their sloppy copy will become neater and easier to read. They will improve upon their ability to put stories in proper sequence and use more complex sentences in the process. As the old saying goes, "practice makes perfect."

MAKING JOURNALS INTO BOOKS

A student has successfully written an interesting story, one that is worthy of being shared with other youngsters besides the sharing done within the classroom or at home. How do you preserve the story? How do you show the child that what has been written is good and that it should not just be filed away and never shared again? The answer to that question is, among other ideas, to "publish" it. There are several simple ways to do this.

CLOTHBOUND BOOKS

If you can get your hands on a few simple materials, you can create colorful books from some of the stories your students write. The materials you will need are:

legal-sized typing paper
cardboard pieces (7" x 8" is a good size)

From *Daily Journals*, published by GoodYearBooks. Copyright © 1993 Carol Simpson.

wallpaper pieces (6" x 14" will fit above cardboard nicely)
fabric swatches (at least 13" x 20" to fit above size)
Tacky Glue® (which can be purchased at fabric stores)
sewing machine, or a swing-away stapler that allows you to staple
in the center fold of the book you are putting together

To bind a cloth-cover book:

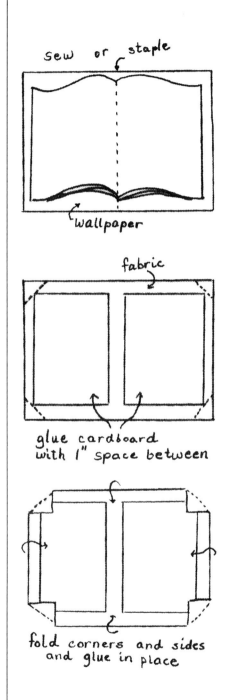

1. Pre-read the story to get the ideas presented. Determine the number of pages needed for copying the complete story. Keep in mind that each sheet of typing paper becomes four pages of the book when folded and fastened together.

2 Be sure to include extra sheets for the title page and a dedication, if wanted. For example, if the number of written and illustrated pages in the child's story is 12, then you will need 4 sheets of typing paper to fold and fasten. Place any blank pages at the end of the book.

3. Select two pieces of cardboard, a piece of fabric, and a piece of wallpaper, all of the correct size needed.

4. Place the wallpaper design-side-up on the table. Center the typing paper sheets on the wallpaper. Center fold the wallpaper and typing paper. Fasten in the center, either by sewing or by stapling with a swing-away stapler. Set this aside for later use.

5. Place the fabric design-side-down on the table. Place the two pieces of cardboard on the cloth so that there is an inch between them and extra fabric on all four sides for folding over the cardboard.

6. Glue the cardboard pieces in place.

7. Fold the cloth edges over the cardboard and glue in place.

8. Center the wallpaper and typing-paper pages on the cardboard and cloth cover, and glue in place.

9. Draw writing lines on the pages, as needed, so that the child can copy and illustrate the story in the cloth book. (If you have a primary typewriter, you might type the words for the children. All they need to do to finish the book is draw the illustrations.)

Because it gets expensive keeping a supply of cloth on hand, you might need to ask your parents to send any excess fabric they have on hand. Let parents know that you require small pieces of cloth and they will usually help out if they can, especially when they see the cloth books their own children are bringing home to keep. The cloth books become real treasures.

COMPUTER TYPED BOOKS

The directions for making cloth books suggest that you make lines with a ruler for the children to copy their stories in their own handwriting. This makes the stories more personal. However, it takes time, and children, especially kindergartners and first-graders, often tire of writing their stories another time. The teacher can elect to type the stories on a computer, word processor, or primary-size typewriter. Cut the sentences or paragraphs that belong on a single page and glue them in their proper places. Then the child needs only to illustrate the pages to finish the product.

VARIATIONS ON THE CLOTH COVER

You will find that using cloth-cover books as a reward for good story writing will encourage your students to want to write more. But because it does get expensive and time consuming, you need to know some other alternatives.

WALLPAPER BOOKS   To make these books, replace the fabric in the cloth book directions with wallpaper. Wallpaper sample books do not supply you with large enough pieces of paper, as a rule, to make covers, so you will need to get rolls instead. Wallpaper stores are often willing to give away two or three rolls of less popular designs. The heavier the wallpaper, the better job it does of holding together as a book cover. However, if you use the same rolls of wallpaper, or only a few patterns from which to choose, everyone's book covers will look about the same!

From *Daily Journals*, published by GoodYearBooks. Copyright © 1993 Carol Simpson.

With cloth, you get a variety of covers. Have children use permanent markers to decorate wallpaper covers with a title and simple picture.

CONTACT-PAPER® BOOKS Yet another variation of the cloth book requires that you substitute Contact Paper® for the fabric cover. This alternative is also a big expense but it is colorful! In addition, Contact Paper® covers eliminate the use of Tacky Glue®. Ask parents if they can donate a roll of contact paper once during the year and you will have plenty to last a long time.

SPIRALBOUND BOOKS Your school P.T.A. might be asked to purchase a special machine that puts a plastic spiral binding on your children's work. The machine punches holes along the left edge of the pages of a story as well as front and back lightweight cardboard covers. Books can be of any size, from a very small book up to 8-1/2" x 11" typing paper. The cardboard covers can be made out of poster weight board of numerous colors. The stories can easily be typed before being put together in the binding. The authors can be given the option of designing cover pictures which can be glued in place to spruce up the front. You might suggest that they incorporate the title of their book in this cover illustration. Although not as long lasting as the cloth/Contact Paper®/wallpaper books described, the spiral bound books will still be works of joy. The children will delight in sharing them with friends and family.

MARY

SPECIAL ADD-ON PAGES Regardless of which type of binding you elect to try, you make the students feel extra proud of their accomplishments if you will add two special pages: a dedication page, and a page that tells all about the author. Students know that real authors have these pages in their books. Real authors like to dedicate their books to special people, and so will your students. Real authors like to tell the reader a little bit about themselves (why they wrote this book, what they like to do in their spare time, etc). Your students will enjoy writing about their families, what they like to do in their free time, their favorite subject in school, as well as their age, grade level, and classroom teacher's name.

STUDENT PRIDE

If you will make cloth, wallpaper, Contact Paper®, or spiralbound books, you will soon discover just how much they mean to the young authors. Once the first few are completed and shared, everyone else wants to get into the act. The pride in the accomplishment is catching. Other children truly enjoy reading the books that their peers write, especially when they are done so colorfully! Parents are always pleased with the books. They become keepsakes and are placed on the bookshelf at home and shown to friends and relatives. The young author gets a deserved pat on the back each time someone sees the book. The experience is very rewarding so the child wants to do it again and again.

USING PARENT VOLUNTEERS

If you plan to do story binding, regardless of the type you choose, you might find it helpful to enlist the aid of a few parent volunteers. Once the idea of publishing stories has caught on, you will need help putting all the books together! If you can get other faculty members interested in creative writing, you can ask parents of students of all grade levels to devote an hour or two each week to setting up a "school publishing center" where all children can send their edited stories to be typed and bound.

Have your students design a school publishing center logo. Make it a contest, with the winner getting a special surprise. It is easy to get your school's simple logo made into a rubber stamp. The logo can then be stamped inside the cover of every book that gets "published" in the center.

PUTTING STUDENTS' WRITING ABILITY TO GOOD USE

The amount of writing children will do depends heavily upon their enjoyment of the activity. This enjoyment is related to the amount of positive feedback received from peers and family when the finished product is presented for their inspection. What is done with the stories to show that the work is worthy of the time it takes to do a good job is an important motivator for most children. Binding stories is one positive way to inspire students, but teachers may decide to do other things as well. Here are a few suggestions.

BOOKS AS HOLIDAY GIFTS

Clothbound books can be used during the school year as gifts. A personally written book makes a very special gift for mom on

ALEX

From *Daily Journals*, published by GoodYearBooks. Copyright © 1993 Carol Simpson.

Mother's Day, a good friend on their birthday, or a grandparent for Christmas, just to name a few. The children see how much grown-ups enjoy their stories and the idea of making a book for a present seems to be a very good one, one worth the time it takes. Children know that their books are going to be shown to friends and family because they are special treasures, they are written from the heart.

USING STORIES FOR PLAYS OR PUPPET SHOWS

A student who has written a good story will feel rewarded for a job well done if that story is used as the basis for a play or puppet show. With a little bit of help from the teacher a good plot can be turned into a script with dialogue for several characters and a narrator.

Kindergartners will probably not create characters or plots that are strong enough for this activity; however, they will enjoy being invited to first-, second-, or third-grade classrooms to see the plays or puppet shows that result from a good story.

If a first-grader has written a strong story, you might want to try to put the basic ideas in dialogue form. The child will need to be involved in the selection of people to play the parts that are written into the story. Unless the child is a gifted writer, the process of turning a plot into dialogue will be much too difficult to understand at this time.

Second- and third-graders are more capable of working in pairs or small groups to create stories with dialogue that would make good plays or puppet shows. By second and third grade, the children have probably had the experience of doing plays or puppet shows and have some understanding of dialogue.

The author(s) of a play or puppet show should be allowed to select players. Allow time for rehearsals so that the players can perform the story for an audience of peers and younger children. If possible, invite parents to get involved in the production. If not, perhaps volunteers could help with making puppets, costumes, setting, puppet theater, props, etc. It is a lot of work to put on a play or puppet show, but the children involved feel much pride in their accomplishment.

MEGAN

STUDENT STORIES AS READING ASSIGNMENTS

A story that is well written and done on a suitable vocabulary level can be used as a reading class assignment. Whether it is done for a small homogeneous reading group or for whole group instruction, everyone involved should be given a copy of the story. The student author gets to be the "teacher" and introduce the story and tell about the plot. The readers can ask the author direct questions about the characters and how they were created, or where the writer got the idea for the story. Put the writer in the "author's chair" for an interview!

STUDENT-MADE WORKSHEETS

A student can play "teacher" and give the class instructions on how to do a child-created worksheet. Children can make their own fill-in-the-blanks, word hunts, scrambled words, or scrambled sentences for their classmates to try. Let the child give directions, grade the papers, and hand them back when checked. To get this type of activity started, you will probably need to suggest that someone make a specific type of worksheet for you; run it off on the copy machine for everyone, and let the child take over the instruction. Once the first student has done this, others will want to try their hand at making a class worksheet! The children love to be the teacher; they love to have the job of grading the papers.

THE LAST WORD

Journal writing takes time; it takes persistence; it requires patience in listening to stories of all levels that are eagerly shared by their authors. Journal writing is worth the time, persistence, and patience. If you will provide the paper and the time, you can get your students to write. You will probably not need to use the variety of story starters provided in this book. Your children will already know what they want to write, especially if they have written journals in previous years. You might just be surprised at how many of them truly enjoy story writing. Give it a try!

ERIN

From *Daily Journals*, published by GoodYearBooks. Copyright © 1993 Carol Simpson.

APPENDIX

The most important (and thrilling) part of the daily writing process is examining the results of the effort you and the children have put forward. Not everyone writes a good story from the beginning. Most early samples are discouraging and may make one think that it isn't worth the time and effort. The examples in this Appendix will hopefully encourage you to continue the daily writing process so that you will see the progress your own children make. Your students will begin to write good stories that you will eagerly share with your colleagues as you begin to see the rewards of your persistence.

REID: FROM TWO LETTERS TO A WHOLE PAGE OF WRITING

Figure 1 is typical for a first-grader who had not tried to write stories before this experience. The September date indicates how early in the year this is. Daily journal writing had been included for at least two weeks. Reid had been drawing pictures and not writing any words. His attempts to write about this picture resulted in two letters, capital *F* and backwards *g*, which stands for the words "football game." The rest of the scribble writing is unreadable, but it probably represents something about playing football and having fun. Not only is Reid's story immature, but his handwriting and stick person also indicate a need for more experiences with crayons and pencils.

Figure 2 shows what Reid is doing near the middle of first grade (February). He is not yet ready to invent the spelling of very many of his words. At this point he is relying on his personal dictionary to spell words correctly so that someone can read his story. Handwriting and illustrations have matured nicely.

9-10-90

Fa

FIGURE 1

Stuart and I
IM uayback
Stuart mud
a goal

2-13-91

FIGURE 2

FIGURE 3

Reid

My Mom and I play basball
We Have Fun together than we
What in to mopping together it was
fun than We wat up star to tac
past than We tuc a woc together
than We played socr it was fun
then it was geted dock
then Mom sed I cud slep in
her room Wen I got up I f
lot of Moms Bad then I Sed
Wer am I she sed home then
I remembd then when I'm in
school

Figure 3 shows the pleasant changes that have taken place by the end of the year. Reid wrote this story about his mother after the class talked about mothers and what they do for us. His story has a nice flow from beginning to middle to end. His attempts at inventing his own spelling are showing improvement. Although his sentences do not contain correct capital letters or punctuation marks, he has not let this stop him from telling a more interesting story. Reid seems to understand that when it comes to story writing, the story idea is more important than the mechanics at this point. Mechanics will improve with practice.

BRIAN: A FEARFUL SPELLER MAKES PROGRESS

When Brian began journals he was afraid to write any words that he could not yet spell. He was not yet sure of the sounds the letters make and therefore was not willing to make mistakes by trying to invent the words. The first-grade curriculum contains a weekly spelling list, beginning about the second week of school. In Figure 4, Brian writes words he knows he can spell. This particular example is typical of every page written in this journal. "I go to" appeared on each page along with a different picture. When Brian shared this journal, he read "I go to surfing." Because each page had a different picture, the last word changed each time and he was pleased with the "story" he had written.

In Figure 5, we see the beginning of Brian's attempts to invent his own spelling. The word "rescuers" is not easy to read, but at least he made the attempt to write it. Brian is making progress. This example is but one page of a journal that told a simple story about rescuing someone from the water. No longer do we find only words he knows he can spell. Each page contains different text instead of all being the same.

A final example of Brian's work comes from the spring of his first-grade year. Brian is gaining confidence in his ability to put down words that tell an interesting story. Confidence is important for children, and daily journals play an important part in confidence building. Even though the progress Brian has made is not dramatic, he has learned a great deal. If his future teachers take the time to let him write each day, he will complete his formal education and become a competent writer. Everyone needs to feel confi-

FIGURE 4

FIGURE 5

FIGURE 6

From *Daily Journals*, published by GoodYearBooks. Copyright © 1993 Carol Simpson.

FIGURE 7

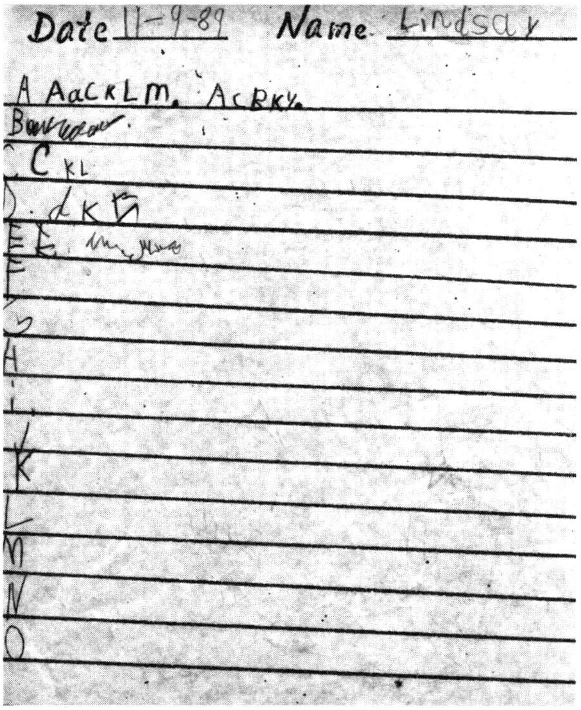

Date 11-9-89   Name Lindsay

A AacKLm, AcRKy.
Baw
C KL
D dkK
E my

FIGURE 9

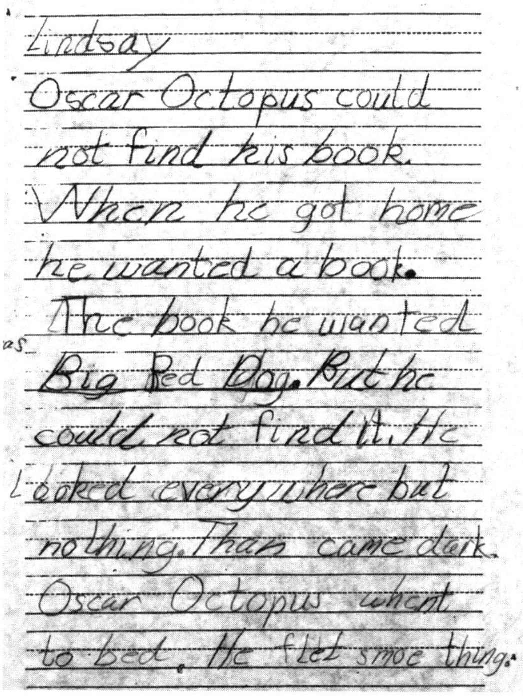

Lindsay
Oscar Octopus could
not find his book.
When he got home
he wanted a book.
The book he wanted
Big Red Dog. But he
could not find it. He
Looked everywhere but
nothing. Then came dark.
Oscar Octopus whent
to bed. He flet smoe thing.

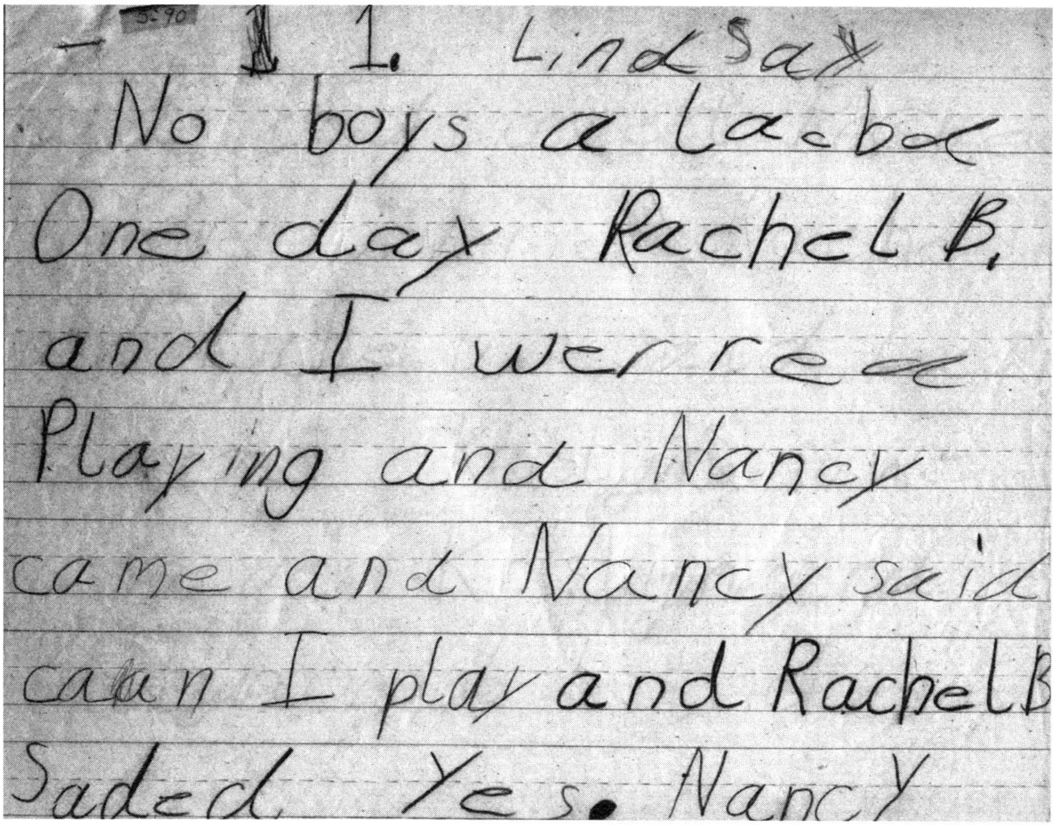

FIGURE 8

1. Lindsay
No boys a lacbd
One day Rachel B.
and I werre
Playing and Nancy
came and Nancy said
caun I play and RachelB
Saded Yes. NancY

dent that they can write a sentence that is complete and correct. Brian should be able to do this. Figure 6 shows that he can write several complete sentences in a sequential order that makes sense. He just needs to work on improving his other written language skills.

LINDSAY: A SHORT ATTENTION SPAN SHOWS IMPROVEMENT

Lindsay had no prior journal writing experience before first grade. She had difficulty writing anything but scribbles because she was impatient. No one had more desire to write a story than Lindsay. During sharing time she would "read" her journal. The stories always got favorable responses from her audience. This positive reinforcement from her peers kept her interested in journal writing, even though Figure 7 shows the typical results of her attempts during the first half of first grade. Lindsay had a long way to go.

In May of first grade, Lindsay wrote "No Boys Allowed." Figure 8 shows the tremendous effort she had to put forth to write a story. The transition from scribble writing to this result came rather suddenly when Lindsay realized that the school year was nearly finished and she did not have a cloth book to keep. The desire to write a story was very strong. She spent many days writing. Even though there is much repetition and many very long sentences with lots of "and's," the story was put in a cloth book. Lindsay could not have been more pleased.

Figure 9 shows Lindsay's writing in second grade. Journal writing is not a part of the daily schedule; creative writing is done, instead, about once a week. The topic is assigned rather than an individual choice. The sample shows that Lindsay can now write a good story with correct punctuation and no running sentences. Lindsay continues to improve nicely. Her short attention span is increasing along with her confidence.

MIKE: DETERMINATION HAS ITS REWARDS

Figures 10 and 11 show the great amount of improvement that can be made when a first-grader wants to write a story but just can't get excited about any subject. Figure 10 is a page of mostly garbled writing (except for the "Go away. I do not want to play."). It is a sharp contrast to the amount of writing Mike did just weeks later, when he wrote

From *Daily Journals*, published by GoodYearBooks. Copyright © 1993 Carol Simpson.

FIGURE 10

12-20-89   god we do
not wet to pA is fter
yos Cat is Cr god god
&Iok kaA HoH wiH
&A1

FIGURE 11

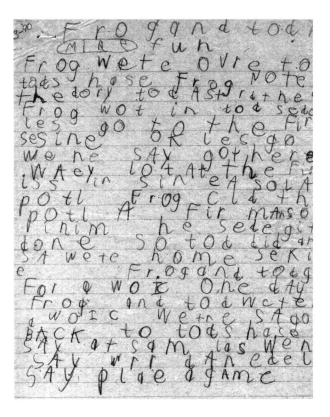

FIGURE 12

By then it was time for supper so we ate. Then we went to bed. While we were in bed, the wind outside blew all the wreaths off the door. The tree still had a snake in it because the place where we got it was a forest. It crawled out and right into my room and in my closet.

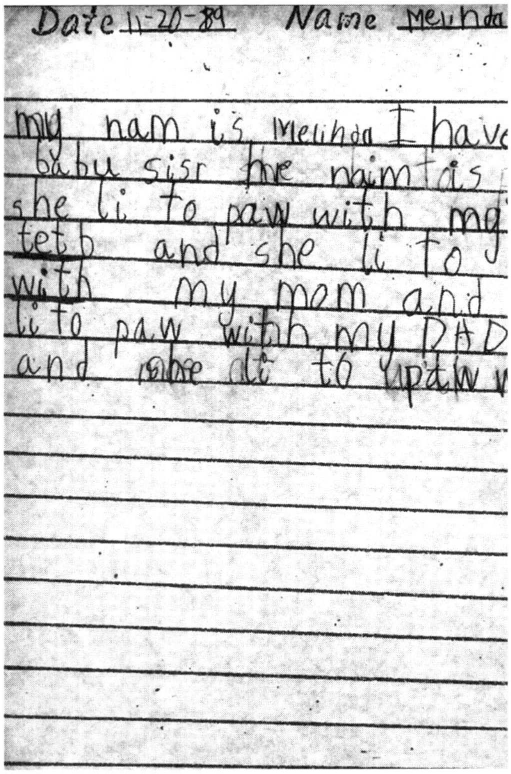

Date 11-20-89 Name Melinda

my nam is Melinda I have
babu sisr her naim is
she li to paw with my
teth and she li to
with my mom and
li to paw with my DAD
and she li to paw

FIGURE 13

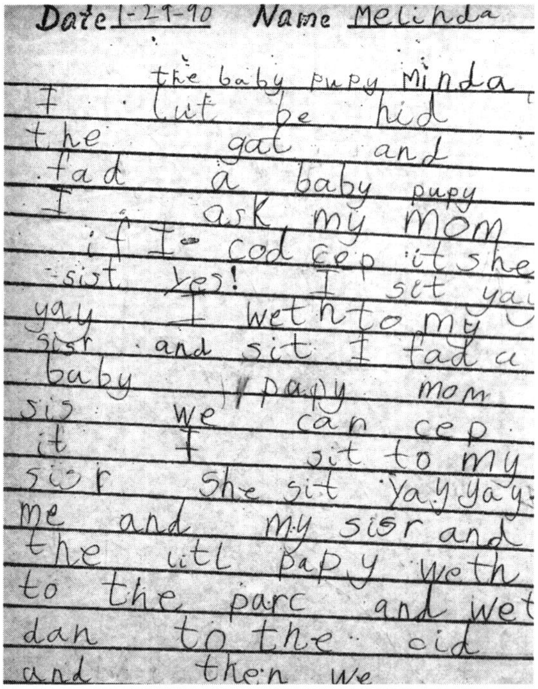

Date 1-29-90 Name Melinda

the baby pupy Minda
I lut be hid
the gat and
fad a baby pupy
I ask my mom
if I cod cep it she
sist yes! I sit yay
yay I weth to my
sisr and sit I fad a
baby pupy mom
sis we can cep
it I sit to my
sisr She sit yay yay
me and my sisr and
the litl papy weth
to the parc and wet
dan to the sid
and then we

FIGURE 14

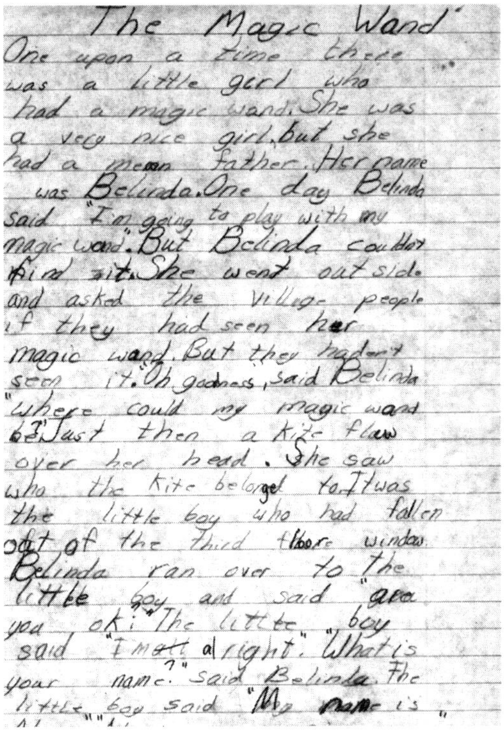

The Magic Wand

One upon a time there
was a little girl who
had a magic wand. She was
a very nice girl, but she
had a mean father. Her name
was Belinda. One day Belinda
said "I'm going to play with my
magic wand." But Belinda couldn't
find it. She went out side
and asked the village people
if they had seen her
magic wand. But they hadn't
seen it. "Oh goodness," said Belinda
"where could my magic wand
be?" Just then a kite flew
over her head. She saw
who the kite belonged to. It was
the little boy who had fallen
out of the third floor window.
Belinda ran over to the
little boy and said "are
you ok?" The little boy
said "I'm all alright." "What is
your name?" said Belinda. The
little boy said "My name is"

FIGURE 15

Figure 11, a story about a frog and toad. The popular Arnold Lobel books about Frog and Toad always have five stories. The simple stories tell of two friends having a good time together, helping each other, and looking out for each other's feelings. Mike has also written five stories about two very good friends. It is obvious that Mike found a subject about which he could enjoy writing. His five stories were combined in his first cloth book. He could not have been more proud when he finished his big writing project.

In third grade, Mike is able to write stories such as Figure 12. This example tells the story of a snake in the Christmas tree! The teacher assigned the topic and then let the children write stories (fact or fiction) about their previous Christmas. Mike's story shows much imagination. He is improving in his ability to write his own story without copying someone else's characters or style.

MELINDA: NO FEAR OF WRITING

Melinda started first grade having no fear of story writing. She always had a writing topic, usually family related. Figure 13 is a good example of her early work. Her little sister is very important to her and is often included in her writing. In this early sample there are no punctuation marks or correct capital letters, but you will notice that most of her sentences are short and complete, except the last one which runs on with many "and's."

By the middle of first grade Melinda is showing that she does not need to write "and" over and over in run-on sentences. Although there is only one correct punctuation mark (the exclamation mark), Figure 14 shows that Melinda will use them when she understands how and when to do so.

In third grade Melinda is not writing daily journals but is being asked to write specific assignments by her teacher. Figure 15 is a story about "magic." Melinda chose to write about a magic wand. The teacher has had an editing conference with her and has helped her correct some of her errors right on the story paper. Melinda still needs to work on improving her punctuation and capitalization. These skills require a lot of practice. They are not learned easily.

FIGURE 16

THE WOS WaSQiYiT

1-22-91

FIGURE 16

TIN THE LITL DED WODDIN TO A DEFR RIT PR

1-25-91

FIGURE 17

She Whent to a Valey of Flying Hosis She Whard Up to The Letear In The Dists.

From *Daily Journals*, published by GoodYearBooks. Copyright © 1993 Carol Simpson.

 APPENDIX

ERIN: A GIFTED WRITER

In kindergarten Erin wrote "The woods was quiet. Because a little fawn was wondering. The fawn was scared of the noises. Then the little deer wandered to a different part." Not many kindergartners are capable of writing a story such as this! Figure 16 shows that it was only the middle of the kindergarten year. Invented spelling had been introduced by the teacher and most children wrote only the first letter of a word and were satisfied. Erin does an excellent job of inventing multisyllabic words ("qiyit" or "dffrrits"). Her illustrations are very detailed for someone her age. Her use of creative colorful language is wonderful!

In first grade Erin continues to create her own stories without prompting from the teacher. "The Magek Unuakorn" (Figure 17) is a good example of her creative ability. Her invented spelling is nearing perfection. She uses the apostrophe in contractions, an occasional period, and the three dots to make a sentence continue on to the next page when she runs out of writing space. Erin is not afraid to try to use the written language skills that have been introduced.

FIGURE 17

She is a prolific reader who practices what she learns in books in her own story writing.

KELLY, MARY, AND STUART: TRUE LIFE BECOMES A JOURNAL STORY

Figures 18 and 19 are perfect examples of stories written from first-hand experiences. Kelly writes about her visit to the dentist's office; Mary's experience has to do with the birth of her new baby brother. Both stories are well written and show a good understanding of sequencing and plot. Stories written about real life events are easier for students to write because they don't have to use their imaginations to create events and characters. When possible, the teacher should encourage students to write about such personal events as the birth of a new baby, a hospital visit, a dentist appointment, marching in a parade, getting a new pet, and others. The teacher knows when something exciting (or troubling) is on a child's mind. Have that child write about it!

Figure 20 tells about a trip to Florida that Stuart took. He was very excited about flying on an airplane and playing on the beach. As a first-grader he wrote this very nice true story.

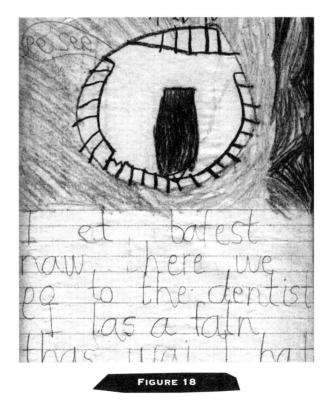

FIGURE 18

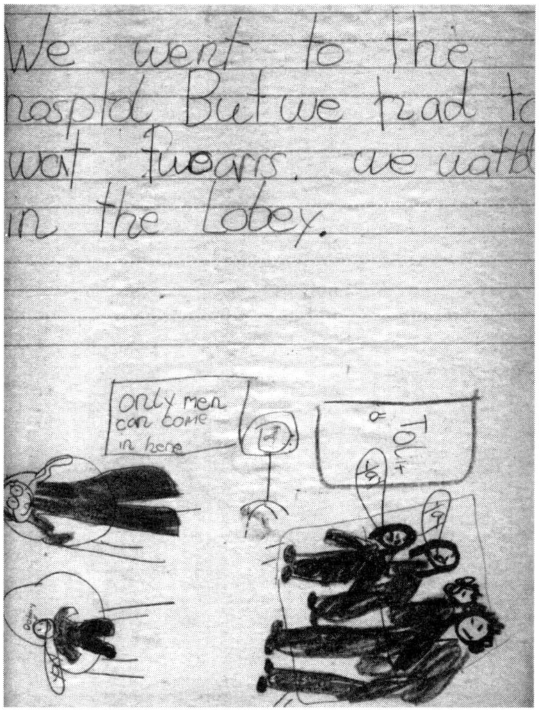
We went to the
hosptal But we had to
wat twoarrs. we watd
in the Lobey.
only men can come in here
Tolit

FIGURE 19

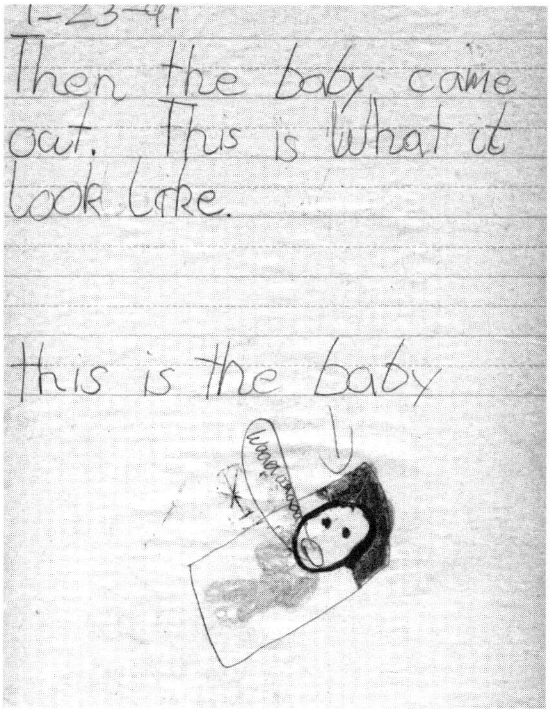
1-23-91
Then the baby came
out. This is what it
look like.
this is the baby

FIGURE 19

FIGURE 20

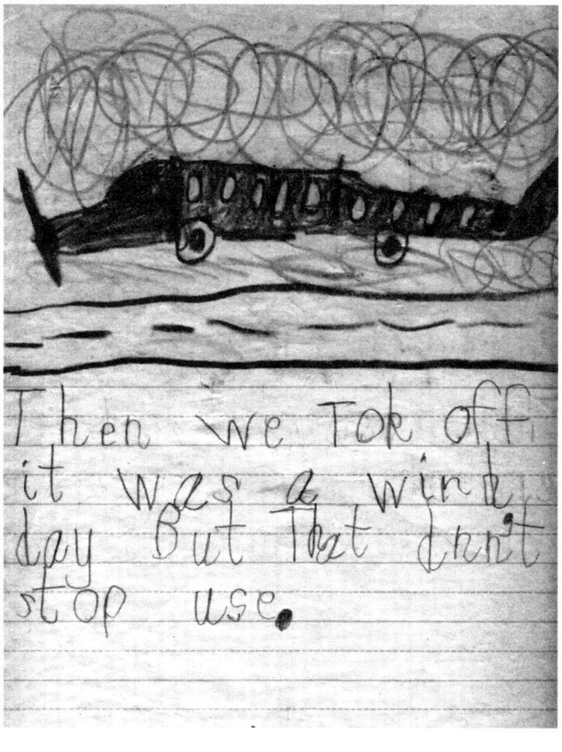
Then we Tok off
it was a wind
day But That dint
stop use.

WRITING ABOUT A SPECIFIC TOPIC

There will be times when teachers will want to assign specific writing topics rather than allowing their students the freedom to write about anything. Many story starters have been provided in this book for just such occasions. Some of them can be used at any time and others will be appropriate during certain holidays or seasons. The remaining student examples are the results of assigned writing topics.

May brings a very special holiday for youngsters. Mother's Day is a wonderful excuse for writing a special story from the heart. Figure 21 shows Brandon's special story. This, and all Mother's Day stories, get bound in colorful cloth covers and become special keepsakes for those lucky moms who receive them.

On page 106, you will find a story starter based on predicting a story after having been given isolated words and phrases from an actual book. The example is from Lois Grambling's *An Alligator Named . . . Alligator* (see page 28). Figures 22, 23 and 24 show what Erin, a first-grader, Kelly, a second-grader, and Ryan, a third-grader, could do when asked to perform this task. These examples show imagination. There are similarities in the three stories, and yet the plots are not the same. All three students were able to write good stories that came close to, but did not match, the original book. After completing the writing, the students got to read Lois Grambling's version, which they enjoyed.

There are many more examples that could have been included within the pages of this book. Hopefully, you will soon have your own collection of children's stories to support the idea that journal writing should have a place in the daily classroom schedule.

From *Daily Journals*, published by GoodYearBooks. Copyright © 1993 Carol Simpson.

Elmo wanted an alligator. His sister said, "You're crazy !!!" Elmo decided not to tell. "Egads!" yelled Elmo's father. "Ther is an alligator doing laps in the swiming pool! Out! out! out!" bye. Elmo waved goodbye. He had to take the alligator to the zoo.

FIGURE 22

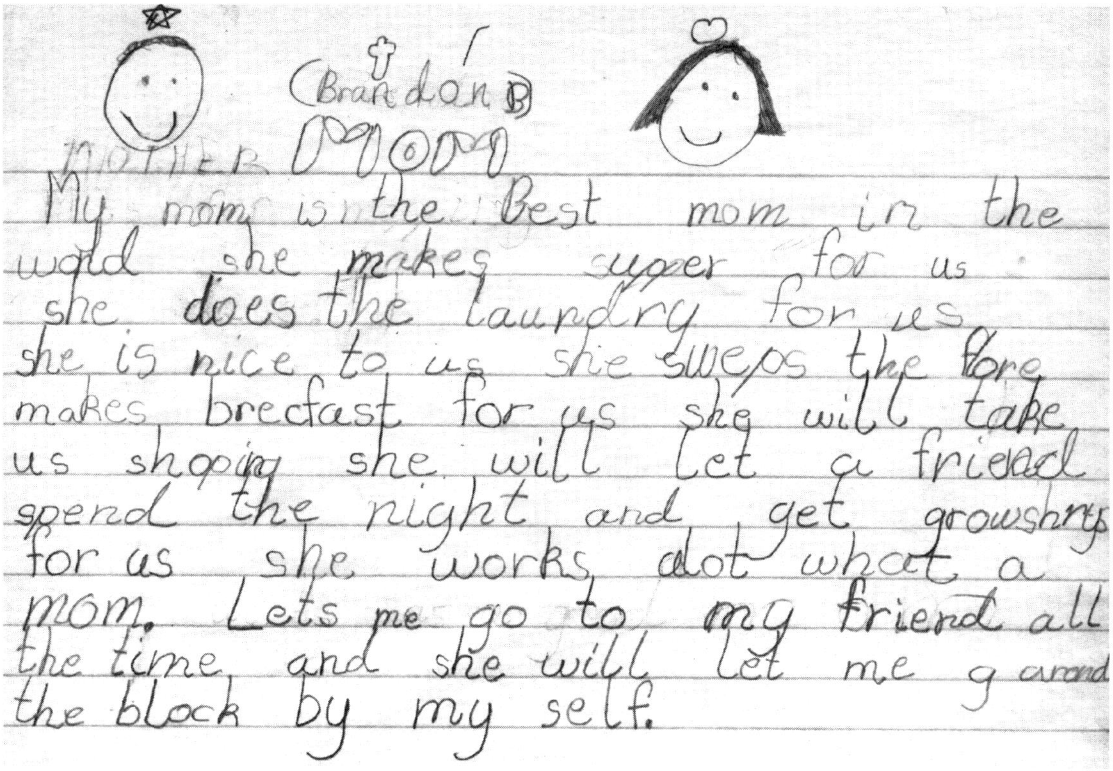

Brandon B

MOTHER MOM

My mom is the best mom in the wold she makes super for us she does the laundry for us she is nice to us she sweps the flore makes brecfast for us she will take us shoping she will let a friend spend the night and get growshrys for us she works dot what a mom. Lets me go to my friend all the time and she will let me g around the block by my self.

FIGURE 21

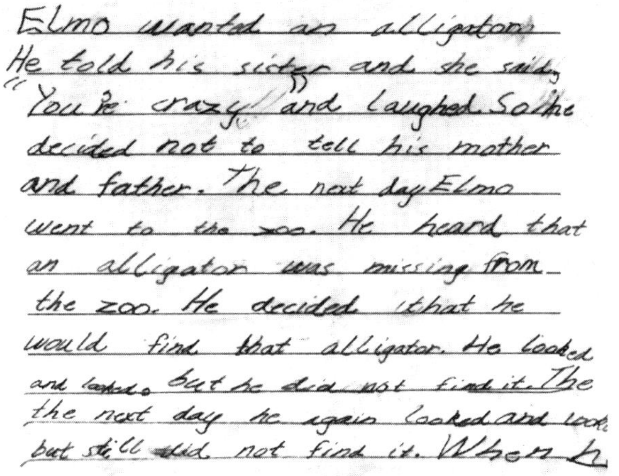

Elmo wanted an alligator. He told his sister and she said, "You're crazy!" and laughed. So he decided not to tell his mother and father. The next day Elmo went to the zoo. He heard that an alligator was missing from the zoo. He decided that he would find that alligator. He looked and looked, but he did not find it. The next day he again looked and looked, but still did not find it. When h

FIGURE 23

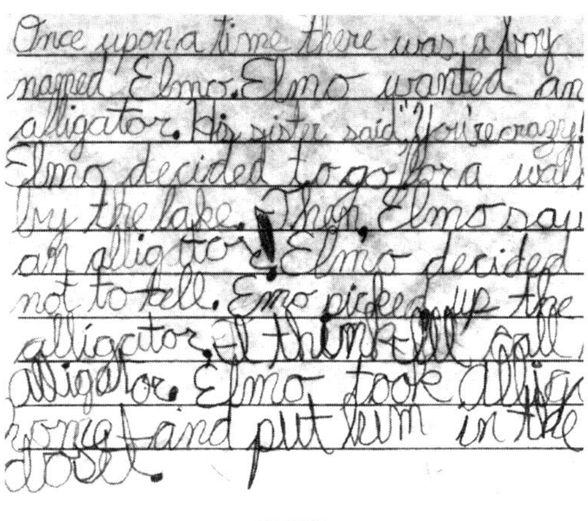

Once upon a time there was a boy named Elmo. Elmo wanted an alligator. His sister said "You're crazy!" Elmo decided to go for a walk by the lake. Then Elmo saw an alligator! Elmo decided not to tell. Elmo picked up the alligator. I think I'll call alligator. Elmo took alligator home and put him in the closet

FIGURE 24

BIBLIOGRAPHY

CHILDREN'S BOOKS

All About Sam by Lois Lowry. New York: Dell Publishing Company, 1988.

Amelia Bedelia books by Peggy Parish. New York: Avon Books, 1963.

An Alligator Named . . . Alligator by Lois G. Grambling. New York: Barron's, 1991.

Animalia by Graeme Base. New York: Scholastic, 1986.

Arthur's Halloween by Marc Brown. New York: Trumpet Club, 1980. (Part of a series on Arthur.)

Brown Bear, Brown Bear, What Do You See? by Bill Martin, Jr. New York: Henry Holt and Company, 1967.

Buzz Buzz Buzz by Byron Barton. New York: Scholastic, 1973.

Chicken Soup with Rice by Maurice Sendak. New York: Scholastic, 1962.

A Chocolate Moose for Dinner by Fred Gwynne. New York: Windmill Books, 1976.

The Doorbell Rang by Pat Hutchins. New York: Mulberry Books, 1986.

Fish Eyes: A Book You Can Count On by Lois Ehlert. New York: Harcourt Brace Jovanovich, 1990.

Fortunately by Remy Charlip. New York: Four Winds, 1964.

Frog and Toad Together by Arnold Lobel. New York: Harper & Row, 1972. (Part of a series on Frog and Toad.)

The Grouchy Ladybug by Eric Carle. New York: Thomas Y. Crowell, 1977.

Harold and the Purple Crayon by Crockett Johnson. New York:

Harper & Row, 1955.

A House for Hermit Crab by Eric Carle. New York: Scholastic, 1987.

"I Can't," Said the Ant by Polly Cameron. New York: Scholastic, 1961.

The Icky Bug Alphabet Book by Jerry Pallotta. Watertown, MA: Charlesbridge, 1986. (Part of a series of alphabet books.)

If the Dinosaurs Came Back by Bernard Most. New York: Harcourt Brace Jovanovich, 1978.

If You Give a Mouse a Cookie by Laura Numeroff. New York: Scholastic, 1985.

I Know an Old Lady by Rose Bonne. New York: Scholastic, 1961.

The Important Book by Margaret Wise Brown. New York: Harper & Row, 1949.

Ira Sleeps Over by Bernard Waber. New York: Scholastic, 1972.

I Went Walking by Sue Williams. New York: Harcourt Brace Jovanovich, 1989.

The Jolly Postman by Janet and Allen Ahlberg. Boston: Little, Brown, 1986.

Little Critter books by Mercer Mayer. New York: Golden Books, 1980-1992.

Little Red Ridinghood by James Marshall. New York: Dial Books, 1987.

The Magic School Bus books by Joanna Cole and Bruce Degen. New York: Scholastic, 1990s.

Miss Nelson books by Harry Allard and James Marshall. New York: Scholastic, 1980s.

The Napping House by Audrey Wood. New York: Harcourt Brace Jovanovich, 1984.

One Sun, a Book of Terse Verse by Bruce McMillan. New York: Scholastic, 1990.

Q Is for Duck by Mary Elting and Michael Folsom. New York: Clarion, 1980.

The Three Wishes by Charles Perrault. Mahwah, NJ: Troll Associates, 1979.

The Very Hungry Caterpillar by Eric Carle. Cleveland: Collins World, 1969.

Wriggles, the Little Wishing Pig by Pauline Watson. New York: Random House, 1978.

Cullinan, Bernice E., editor. *Children's Literature in the Reading Program.* Newark, DE: International Reading Association, 1987. Well-known authors and educators discuss literature and its practical applications in primary and intermediate grade classrooms. Each of the 14 chapters features many teaching ideas.

Eisele, Beverly. *Managing the Whole Language Classroom.* Cypress, CA: Creative Teaching Press, 1991. A desktop reference on: organizing the whole language classroom around centers; daily schedules; practical suggestions for including journal writing; and how to make simple books. The book also includes useful reproducible forms. Used in conjunction with Ms. Eisele's management seminar, this book is an excellent introduction to new classroom organization.

Evans, Joy, and others. *Making Big Books with Children.* Monterey, CA: Evan-Moor, 1989. This 11" x 17" guide to making big books is filled with numerous reproducible patterns and story starters. It is a must for teachers who want to incorporate creative writing in their primary classrooms. Also highly recommended are the Evan-Moor one-day workshops on thematic teaching and other topics of interest to whole language teachers.

Evans, Joy, and Moore, Jo Ellen. *How to Make Books with Children.* Monterey, CA: Evan-Moor, 1985. A wealth of ideas for making books of all shapes, sizes, and types (accordion books, folded books, shape books, and others), along with story-starter ideas to spark the writing process.

Goodman, Ken. *What's Whole in Whole Language.* Portsmouth, NH: Heinemann, 1986. A practical, easy-to-read explanation of the whole language philosophy of teaching language arts. Teachers who are considering the transition should read this book, but parents will also understand the text.

Massam, Joanne, and Kulik, Anne. *And What Else?* Bothell, WA: The Wright Group, 1990. The hundred-plus colorful photos of writing/art ideas actually used in the classroom make this a book you'll look at time and time again for instant inspiration.

The Reading Teacher, The Journal of the International Reading Association. A monthly professional magazine (9 issues per year) with excellent research-based articles covering all aspects of teaching reading and language skills, as well as monthly "departments" that supply readers with practical ideas and introductions to new children's literature.

Rothlein, Liz, and Wild, Terri. *Read It Again!* Glenview, IL: GoodYearBooks, 1989. This series is a good resource for the teacher of the traditional basal approach who would like to begin incorporating literature in reading instruction. Two books include ideas for many favorite K-2 stories and provides reproducible pages that can help young writers organize their own story ideas into a creative writing activity. Other books in the *Read It Again!* series include materials for Pre-K and for grades 3-5.

Routman, Regie. *Transitions.* Portsmouth, NH: Heinemann, 1988. An easy-to-read handbook for any teacher who wants to incorporate whole language techniques in his or her K-3 classroom. It is filled with practical ideas as well as the author's personal classroom experiences.

Sampson, Michael, and others. *Pathways to Literacy.* Fort Worth, TX: Holt, Rinehart and Winston, 1991. A textbook on whole language teaching, this book is the backbone reading material for "Pathways to Literacy" conferences conducted by Bill Martin, Jr. The week-long summer workshops are an excellent source of practical information for anyone interested in learning new methods of teaching language and literacy skills.

Sterling, Mary Ellen. *Making Big and Little Books.* Huntington Beach, CA: Teacher Created Materials, 1991. Dozens of creative ideas for making shape books, accordion books, folded books, and wheel books, with information on how to display them in the classroom. This is an excellent resource for teachers who want to make easy books that don't require extra materials.

Watson, Dorothy, and others. *Whole Language: Inquiring Voices.* New York: Scholastic, 1989. This book explores the idea of allowing children the opportunity to ask questions in order to help fomulate curriculum. Children act as researchers and teachers as facilitators in the learning process.

Yeager, David Clark. *The Whole Language Companion.* Glenview, IL: GoodYearBooks, 1991. Although the cover indicates that this book is aimed at teachers of grades 4-8, it also offers general information that is valuable to teachers of all grade levels. The "Personal Planning Pages" throughout the book afford help to traditional skills-based teachers who would like to move into a whole language approach. The book includes many reproducibles that are helpful to teachers and students alike.

PROFESSIONAL ORGANIZATIONS

International Reading Association
800 Barksdale Road
P. O. Box 8139
Newark, DE 19714-8139

The Whole Language Umbrella
#6-846 Marion Street
Winnipeg, Manitoba, Canada
R2J 0K4